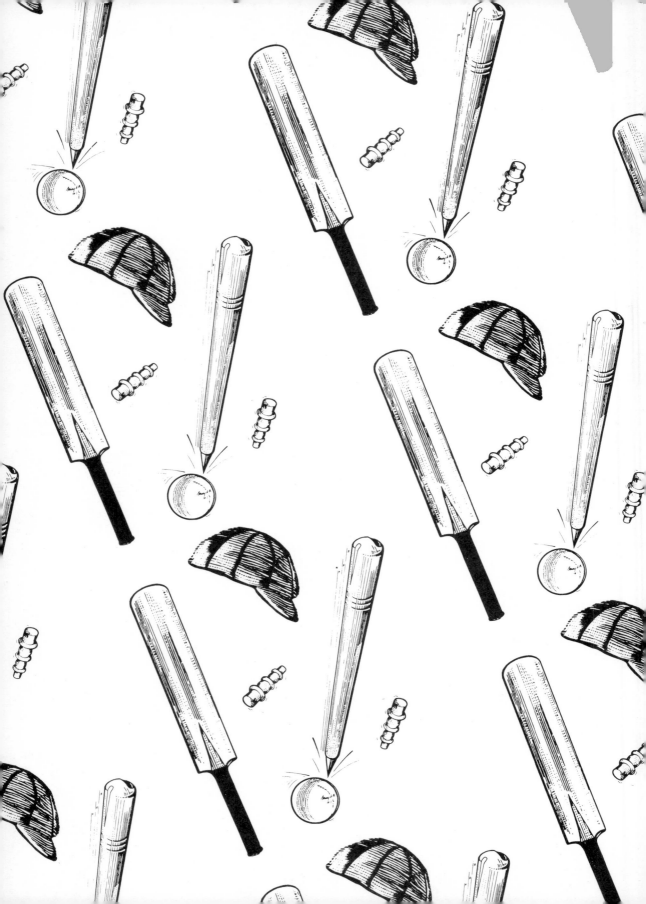

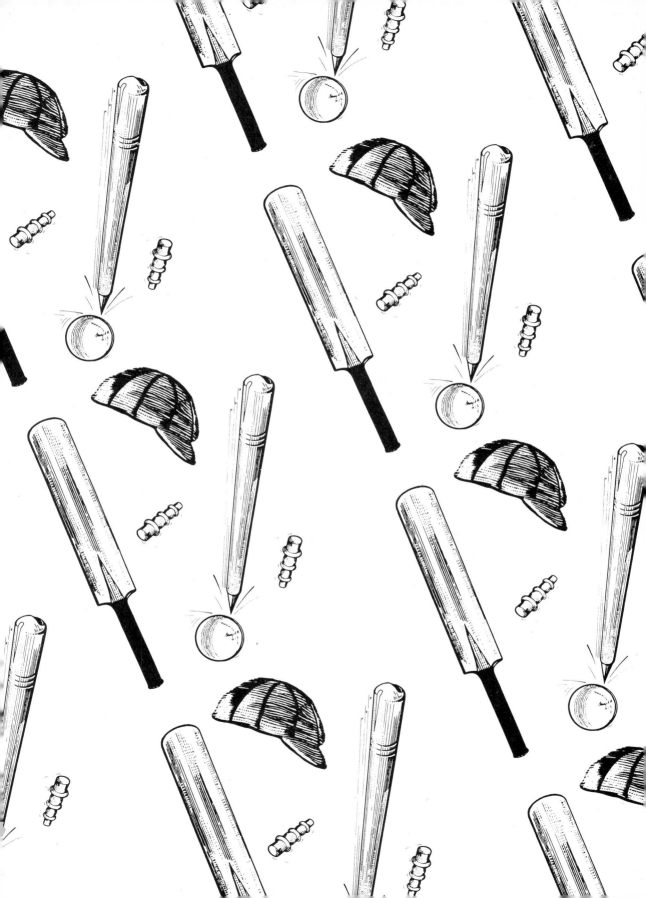

Author Information
Christopher Martin-Jenkins is Editor of The Cricketer and widely known as a cricket commentator. He is also an enthusiastic player of the game and suffered his own personal 'disaster' when he was dismissed on 99 in a school match at Lord's. He went on to play for Surrey 2nd XI and is still active in club cricket. Christopher Martin-Jenkins is also much in demand as an after-dinner speaker. He spends what spare time he has with his wife, two sons and daughter at their home in West Sussex.

The
Cricketer
BOOK
OF
CRICKET
DISASTERS
&
AND
BIZARRE RECORDS

GENERAL EDITOR
CHRISTOPHER MARTIN-JENKINS
INTRODUCTION BY
MIKE BREARLEY
ILLUSTRATIONS BY
S. McMURTRY

CENTURY PUBLISHING
L O N D O N

First published in Great Britain in 1983
by Century Publishing Co. Ltd

First published as a paperback in 1984
by Century Publishing Co. Ltd,
Portland House,
12-13 Greek Street, London W1V 5LE

Second impression 1984
Third impression 1985

ISBN 07126 0908 3

Made by Lennard Books
Mackerye End
Harpenden, Herts AL5 5DR

Compiled by Grahame Thornton
Editor Michael Leitch
Designed by David Pocknell's Company Ltd
Production Reynolds Clark Associates Ltd
Printed and bound in Spain by
TONSA, San Sebastian

CONTENTS

Introduction 6
The Nature of Disaster: A Prologue 10
Bizarre Bowling Records 14
Disasters of Dismissal 24
The Most Violent Game 30
Strangest Venues 36
They Travelled Most Hopefully 42
Bizarre Fielding Records 48
All Ends Up 54
Apocalypse Stopped Play 56
Bizarre Batting Records 60
Bloodthirsty Cricket 66
Bizarre Umpiring Records 68
Most Uncricket-like Performances 72
Bizarre Wicketkeeping Records 76
Breaks in Play 80
Family Connections 88
Most Runs Off One Ball 92
Animal Havoc 94
Bizarre Lines from the Scorebook 98
Most Ancient of Players 104
Most Dramatic Turnarounds 108
Jumping Bails 112
Local Rules 116
Acknowledgments 121

INTRODUCTION

Life is no game of cricket and no sporting disaster is really disastrous, provided that we exclude extraneous catastrophes, of which many cases are to be found in the pages that follow, such as the fielder dashing himself to death from a cliff-edge at the end of an over-enthusiastic chase.

Games, however, like art, achieve their impact in part in the way they reflect and symbolize life outside the frame, the stage, the arena. And of all games, cricket embodies the passions of life most richly.

Cricket can be, for instance, unspeakable, as drab and futile as a fruitless journey. It can also be too brief, ended almost before it has begun. An octogenarian cricket-lover said to me the other day that he lives for the summer and it is already half over. Cricket allows for the draw, a 'result' that has little in common with the tie or the dead-heat. It is both curious and lifelike that a game should exist in which two sides play for the best part of a week without deciding who has won; and that this term 'draw' can be used to describe both an outcome in which neither team is within a mile of winning, and one in which one side has utterly outplayed the other but still requires a single wicket or run.

All games, like life, serve up a variety of blows and ignominies. For every horse that comes from behind for a thrilling win by a nose, there are several that struggle in the heavy going or fall at the first fence, or fade slowly after a promising start. In cricket, for the batsman, virtually every innings implies a loss which, in the context of the game, is absolute. One false shot, a blinding catch, a bizarre moment, and PHUTT! the flame flickers and is out. The batsman has to go; to stop doing that which he came to do. Disaster punctuates the most successful batting careers, not with commas but with full stops – if not exclamation marks!

Cricketing dismissals contain, then, elements of both the disastrous and the absurd. Brian Close had a knack of making his own dismissals amusing. He once said of a ball from Vanburn Holder (from which he was caught and bowled) that he had it covered for everything except bad bounce. In another match his innings lasted only two balls. In the dressing-room, the twelfth man left the statutory orange squash beside his seat and the other players, as was their wont on such occasions, either disappeared altogether or, hiding behind their newspapers, maintained a sombre and funereal silence. Beetling brows furrowed, the great man reached his place, preceded by his bat. He sat down, glaring. There was a brief silence. 'That bloody twelfth man,' he eventually pronounced, 'gave me chewing-gum of t'wrong bloody flavour.'

In a match at Lahore I was once given out caught at the wicket when the ball flicked my pad-strap. The umpire's arm had shot up in response to an appeal launched by more than 30,000 throats. I was not amused, especially as we had fielded for a day and a half, and I had only scored four. My feelings were only partly moderated when I received a message later that day. 'The umpire asks me to tell you,' said the sympathetic liaison officer, 'that he is very sorry, but he felt his arm going up and couldn't stop it.'

For the scorer, these little triumphs and disasters are merely facts, soberly to be received and soberly recorded. I enjoyed this story, a tribute to one scorer's dead-pan sobriety in reaction to a bizarre episode in a match between Leicestershire and Sussex. It was one of those intolerable days when the weather, the setting and the state of the match combined to make the game tedious in the extreme. There was no chance of a result; it was cold; it rained intermittently, but not heavily enough to justify calling the match off. The scorers were virtually the only spectators. John Snow was not a man to feel elated at the thought of bowling in such circumstances; and on one restart, when he was to resume an over that had been interrupted by a shower, he took out of his pocket a bright red soap cricket ball that had caught his eye in the toiletries department of the Leicester Woolworths. His first delivery was a perfect bouncer. The soap ball skidded on the damp grass, just like the original might have done. Peter Marner, the batsman, got perfectly into position and hooked fiercely. The ball shattered into fragments. The Sussex scorer placed an asterisk beside the dot in his book and at the bottom of the page he elaborated briefly on the incident. 'Ball exploded,' he wrote.

Snow was not above a bit of good-humoured chicanery. In one Test the umpire, Dickie Bird, had been forced constantly to hold up play because of the movement of spectators in the pavilion behind the bowler's arm. England were in no hurry to get through their overs, as the West Indies score at tea on the second day was well over 400. After the interval Snow, who was bowling from Bird's end, deposited a pocketful of cake crumbs at the end of his run-up. Birds swooped. Bird panicked. Snow smiled.

Sometimes things get so bad, you can only laugh. I hope you will find plenty to laugh about in this collection of some of the game's bizarre and sometimes disastrous occurrences.

THE Nature OF DISASTER

A PROLOGUE

Most cricket followers know that Don Bradman averaged 99 in Test cricket, and that he might well have averaged 100 if he had not been bowled second ball by Eric Hollies at The Oval in his final Test innings.

Anyone who has played cricket at any level knows that all players have their days of disaster, as well as their days of glory. Nor can anyone, even at those glorious times when the game seems simple because the mind for once dictates that it is, be quite sure whether triumph or disappointment lies round the next corner. A master at Wellington College's Prep School, Eagle House, Richard Parsons (now a successful wine merchant incidentally), was the unfortunate umpire some years ago when the school eleven under his charge was bowled out for one by a rival school. More embarrassed than irritated, he said to his opposite number between innings: 'I'm sorry not to have given your boys much practice. I do assure you my chaps can do much better than this.'

They did. They bowled the opposition out for nought!

Curiously enough, one of my sons made his first appearance in any cricket match in an under-eleven game against the same school, Eagle House. I arrived just in time to see him stride out keenly to take guard. He pushed a gentle catch first ball to silly mid-off and departed, somewhat bemused, for a golden duck or, as we called it at my own prep school, a drake. I consoled him with reminders that Sir Leonard Hutton and others had made nought on their first appearance in a Test Match. Twelve months later young James, now just ten, made 93 not out against the same Eagle House. Whether or not he goes on to be a really good player time will tell, but if he plays much more such ups and downs will be inevitable. Since this is a book mainly about the bizarre and the calamitous, it is worth remembering that the game can be kind and heart-warming as well as cruel and heartless.

The book came about partly because as editor of *The Cricketer* I frequently receive details of curious or remarkable achievements and incidents on the cricket field. Indeed you have only to read Findlay Rea's accounts of the Whitbread Village competition, which is organized by *The Cricketer*, to appreciate how many things happen in real cricket matches which would seem absurd flights of fancy in a work of fiction. Moreover, coincidences abound in the game: only recently I received a letter from an umpire who stood in two games on successive days, both of which ended in a genuine tie.

This is intended to be a lighthearted book, *not* a serious book of records, which readers may feel are not exactly in short supply these days. It has not been possible to authenticate every story, though we have done our best to avoid the occasional examples of amazing performances which Peter Richardson used to invent and send under a false name in the hope of catching E. W. Swanton when he was cricket correspondent of *The Daily Telegraph*. Jim was shrewd enough in most instances to smell a rat and we hope we have been too, but readers are invited to dispute – or cap – any of the stories that follow.

All good stories are in danger of becoming exaggerated or distorted in the telling and there is nothing so imprecise as a cricketer's memory. Nevertheless the stories mentioned here have been included on the basis of fact, even if imagination has sometimes embroidered the tale.

It is extraordinary how many apparently unlikely events on the

cricket field have in fact happened time and again: such bizarre occurrences as birds being struck by cricket balls or boxes of matches catching fire in the pocket of a batsman or fielder. This is one reason why it has not been possible to include all the stories which readers of *The Cricketer*, and others, have kindly sent to us. We are, nonetheless, extremely grateful for their interest and cooperation.

I should like to give special thanks to our contributors from Fiji, Denmark, the United Arab Emirates and Holland as well as from the better known cricketing countries.

All of us have suffered something bizarre on the cricket field if we have played the game for any length of time. Amongst my own memories are overbalancing as I shouldered arms to a leg-break bowler and as a result being stumped first ball; catching someone in my sweater off the first ball of an over whilst I was still in the process of putting it on after bowling the previous over, and being a member of a team which very nearly drew a match played in perfectly fine weather after the side for which I was playing had been bowled out for 13. Our thirteen-year-old captain could have taught Brian Close a thing or two about slowing the game down in the field!

I hope you will find some entertainment in this book about the bizarre and disastrous side of the game and that some of the stories may rekindle memories of your own experiences. If so, please write and tell us. I have no doubt that we have only scratched the surface so far.

Christopher Martin-Jenkins

BIZARRE
BOWLING
RECORDS

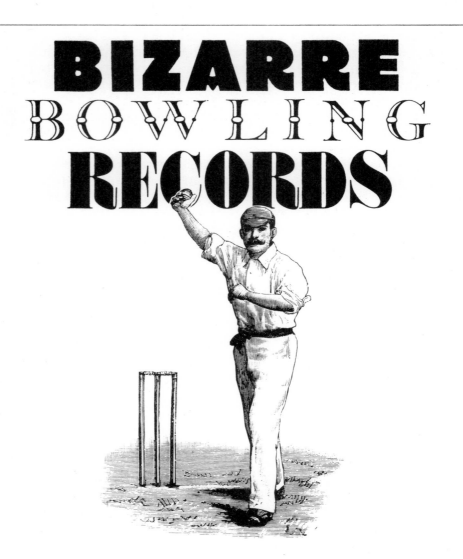

PERFECT PARTNERS

For the batting side under siege from both ends of the pitch, on one of those magical days when each bowler is on song and will not be denied, the battle is one of attrition, and the best that any batsman can hope for is to be the one who is not out at the end of the ordeal.

Contrast their strained faces with the serene expression worn by the captain of the fielding side. Freed from the need to worry about changing his bowlers, he glides effortlessly about, lapping up the experience of having greatness thrust so pleasantly upon him.

The County Championship has thrown up a host of deadly bowling partnerships, and every partisan will have his favourites. Among the most effective Victorians were the Lancashire pair W. McIntyre and A. Watson, who in 1876 bowled unchanged in both matches against Derbyshire, dismissing them for

60 and 78 at Old Trafford and 63 and 125 at Derby. The Lancashire bowlers finished with two-match analyses of 23–168 and 15–146 respectively.

In 1935 G. Geary and H. A. Smith of Leicestershire struck gold in four consecutive innings. Their opponents were shot out for 77, 72, 85 and 79.

In the Bradford League in 1942 Lidget Green barely needed more than two bowlers. A. Bastow, with 63 wickets at 6.96 each, and Tommy Mitchell, 78 wickets at 8.94, took every wicket falling that season to a Lidget Green bowler.

Alfred Mynn, the 'Lion of Kent', in a lithograph by the Victorian artist G. F. Watts, 1845.

MOST DAMAGING BOWLER
Alfred Mynn, the 18-stone 'Lion of Kent', was so fast in his heyday, circa 1840, that his brother was one of the few who would stand at longstop to him. Once, when his brother was not on duty, Mynn struck his longstop in the chest with six consecutive deliveries. This had such a concave effect on the poor man that he had to be taken home where he spat blood for a fortnight.

CAT AND MOUSE
Horace Rochfort, a slow left-arm bowler, was a pioneer of cricket in Ireland in the 1830s. He also had the most stuttering action of his day, and perhaps of any other day. Rochfort's run-up began about ten yards from the wicket, but he could never do the simple thing and reach the crease in continuous strides. Every few steps he stopped, put the ball up to his eye – to see if he was going in the right direction? – and continued his run.

In one match he came up against a certain Lieutenant Ricardo, who with a true gambler's instinct would wait for Rochfort to begin his run-up then go for a stroll round the wicket, returning just in time to play the ball. There was indeed a lot of gambling in the game at that time, and Ricardo's ploy, while extreme, typifies the cavalier approach of some players.

Charles Kortright of Essex, one of the fastest bowlers of all time.

STEEPEST DELIVERY
Charles Kortright, playing at Wallingford, once bowled a ball that rose so steeply that it passed over the batsman and the wicketkeeper and cleared the boundary without bouncing. He thus registered the only incidence of six byes in the history of the game.

THE IRISH SWEEP

Triumph and disaster for bowler Hampton Ewart are recorded in this scorecard of a match in 1972 between Armagh and Portadown. Batting first, Armagh compiled a very forgettable 55, then were mightily cheered by the form of opening bowler Ewart who worked steadily to figures of 8 for 7, at which point he was on a hat-trick. He bowled to N. Alcock who struck the ball in the air and set off down the pitch. The fielder dropped the catch, the batsmen turned for a second run and Alcock was run out. Ewart then disposed of the last two Portadown batsmen for two runs. If the catch had been taken, Ewart might have had 10 wickets for 9 runs instead of 9 for 10.

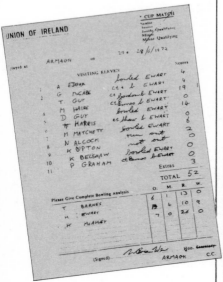

CLEAN SWEEPS

While it must be satisfying to capture all 10 wickets in an innings, how much sweeter by far to take all 20 in a match. No fewer than six instances of this remarkable feat have been recorded. The only one for which we have no date is 'Martin's Massacre' – the match at Common Down, Stockbridge, when a home-side bowler called Martin took all 20 wickets of the opposing side, Abbot's Ann, for 'a little over four runs apiece'.
The others, in date order, were:

Frederick Robert Spofforth, 'the Demon', most famous of the exclusive band of bowlers who have taken all 20 wickets in a match. Cartoon by Spy, published in *Vanity Fair*, 1878.

1881–82. F. R. Spofforth in Australia, in an up-country match to which he is said to have ridden 400 miles in order to take part.
1887. J. Bryant for Erskine v. Deaf Mutes in Melbourne. All were clean-bowled.
1932. Y. S. Ramaswami for Marimallapa High School v. Wesleyan High School, Bangalore, bowling right-arm leg-breaks and googlies for a match analysis of 20–31, including a hat-trick.
1935. W. Doig for Great Fremantle in a match at Perth, Western Australia; he took 10–15 in the first innings and 10–6 in the second.
1950. James Pothecary, aged 16, for Seapoint v. Lansdowne, Cape Town; his match analysis was 20–54.

For all the finite qualities of those figures we cannot refrain from asserting that the greatest 'sweep' of them all was Jim Laker's 19–90 v. Australia at Old Trafford in 1956; in the first innings he took 9–37, in the second 10–53. Had not Cowdrey caught Burke off the bowling of Tony Lock in the first innings – who knows, Laker might have swept the board entirely. At the same time, we feel that Laker's is perhaps *the* cricketing record least likely to be broken.

Descending briefly to the less heady world of 10 wickets in an innings, we find that this has been achieved so many times, a careful listing would have barely more appeal to most readers than scanning a Greek telephone directory. However, if the feat has a champion, he is Azim Khan of Alwar, and ambitious wicket-takers will do well to note that between 1914 and 1927 Azim captured all 10 wickets in an innings no fewer than nine times.

A man who might be forgiven for thinking he had taken 12 wickets in an innings was H. S. Dawe, playing for Tarvin v. Thistleton in 1881. In the course of skittling 10 Thistleton batsmen at a personal cost of 25 runs, Dawe twice produced deliveries which passed between the stumps without removing the bails. Afterwards it was found that the groundsman had gauged the distance between the stumps with an old and swollen ball.

MOST CACKHANDED BOWLERS

Not only on beaches and in gardens can bowlers be seen tossing up deliveries with either hand. In 1954, playing for Pakistan v. Somerset at Taunton, the usually right-armed Hanif Mohammad decided to try each arm in the same over and took a wicket with a left-arm delivery.

In 1872, in the match between Harrow School and Butterflies, the latter's W. Yardley bowled alternately with his right and left arm, and took five wickets.

William Frederick Light (1880–1930) made a habit of it. He was the professional at Exeter and Devon for some twenty years, and opened the bowling with fast-medium left arm. If necessary, he would later switch to slow right arm. Before joining Exeter and Devon he played 12 matches for Hampshire and so may have deployed the same repertoire in the first-class game.

Impressive action.

BEST HAT-TRICKS

In this highly competitive field the ultimate accolade – for a hat-trick of hat-tricks – is shared by two schoolboys. First to bag his nine wickets in nine deliveries was Paul Hugo, playing in Johannesburg for Smithfield v. Aliwal North in 1931. Then in 1967 his feat was emulated by 14-year-old Stephen Fleming, bowling for Marlborough College in Blenheim, New Zealand, against Bohally Intermediate.

The previous record was eight in eight – achieved in 1882 at Ashcombe Park by the home side's professional, known to us only as Walker, who took 9 Turnstall wickets in 11 balls for 0 runs.

Seven wickets in seven balls, while remarkable enough, has not been beyond quite a few cricketers. In Australia, for instance, at least four bowlers have pulled it off. In chronological order they were:

1884–85. F. Howett in South Australia.
1908–09   P. Mossman for Prep School v. Sydney Cape Grammar 2nd XI.
1947–48. M. Perryman for Mossman B, Sydney; he finished with 10 for 6.
1972–73. S. Harding for Wagga Wagga v. Turvey Park.

Nearly as good was a spell by H. F. 'Harry' Boyle, who in 1878 at Leeds took seven wickets in eight balls for Australia v. XVIII of Elland.

In South Africa, seven in seven was achieved in the 1900–01 season by James Dowd, bowling for Stanislaus College, Bathurst. (Five years later he was playing for Orange District against Reserves and clean-bowled all 10 batsmen.)

Still on the seven-in-seven theme, in 1972 two Australian bowlers combined to produce a procession of seven departing batsmen in a second-grade match between Lake Illawarra and Gerrigong. First Gerrigong's David Emery took a wicket with ● each of the last three balls of his over. Then from the other end Brian Arberry sent four batsmen back to the pavilion with consecutive deliveries, and Lake Illawarra had tumbled from 2–30 to 9–30.

Next best is six wickets in seven balls. The bowler was Kevin Sobels, a medium-pacer for B-grade side Muswellbrook Workers, Scone, in a match in 1976 against Senenhoe ABC Bunnen United. He might have had six wickets in six balls, but an l.b.w. appeal was turned down.

The man with the most hat-tricks in a match must be W. Clarke, who for St Augustine's College, Ashford v. Ashford Church Choir in 1912 took three in the choristers' first innings and two in the second.

On 19 June 1983 two bowlers from the same club each achieved a hat-trick on the same day in different matches. Jonathan Elliot, playing for Botany Bay (Middlesex) v. Edmonton, captured three in a row and followed up with 102 not out, including nine sixes, to give his club victory by one wicket. On the same day, playing for the 2nd XI v. Winchmore Hill at Ford's Grove, another Botany Bay bowler, Brian Chetwynd, also did the hat-trick.

At first-class level some astonishing feats have also gone into the scorebooks. In his benefit match in 1922, the Gloucestershire bowler C. W. L. Parker hit the stumps of Yorkshire opponents five times in five balls, though the second was a no-ball. Perhaps the gods smile on beneficiaries, for in his benefit match in 1907 A. E. Trott of Middlesex took four Sussex wickets in four balls and later in the same innings performed the hat-trick. At Leyton in 1920 Essex bowler P. S. E. Toone saw no need for any warm-up deliveries: he took the wickets of Kent batsmen Collins, Woolley and Seymour with his first three balls.

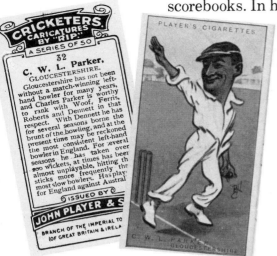

C. W. L. Parker of Gloucestershire, who once hit the stumps with five successive deliveries – though the second was a no-ball.

Most dazzling first-class débutant was South African R. R. Phillips, who in 1939–40 achieved a hat-trick in his first over for Border Province. Most shattering performance was by a Mr Aitken of Sleaford, who in 1892 clean-bowled three batsmen in succession and each time he did so broke a stump. Most barren years for hat-tricks were 1877 and 1954, when none was registered in the first-class County Championship. Most negative hat-trick was that by M. A. Wahind of Moore Sports Club, who in a Daily News Trophy match in Ceylon against Notts Cricket & Athletic Club warned batsman No 8 about backing-up. His conscience thus quieted, in the next three balls he ran out Nos 8, 9 and 10.

FREAK FIGURES

When he was a schoolboy at Brighton College in the 1880s, S. M. J. Woods bowled an over in which he hit the stumps eight times with eight balls but instead of producing a feat to rival that of Mr Walker (see 'Best Hat-tricks', above) he emerged with a haul of only three wickets.

His first three deliveries were no-balls; the fourth bowled a man; the fifth touched the leg-stump and went for byes; the sixth and seventh bowled men; the eighth hit the stumps but failed to remove the bails and went for four more byes.

In May 1980 Curry Rivel bowler Brian Rostill had little reason to think he was on the verge of something special when he conceded 17 runs in his opening eight-ball over against Pitminster, but the next time he took the ball his fortunes were transformed. He took six wickets, all clean-bowled, with, in between, two no-balls which also hit the stumps.

Cricket dancing: pupils at Lilleshall coaching centre in 1952 practise the bowler's waltz, or so it seems, at the start of a new M.C.C. group coaching scheme.

EVERY ONE A COCONUT!

In 1934 a 13-year-old boy played havoc among the coconuts at the fairground in Newport, Isle of Wight. Instead of throwing the ball like a fielder returning it to the stumps, his shies were 'bowled', complete with run-up and action heavily modelled on Harold Larwood. So accurate was he, almost every ball dislodged a coconut. Word spread round the fairground and soon he was being commissioned by strangers to bowl on their behalf. Eventually the stallholder, faced with a near-empty sack, had to bar the boy – but only after he had knocked down 87 fruit of the palm.

KING OF SWERVE

The American fast bowler J. B. 'Bart' King might also have done well at coconut shies with his baseball pitcher delivery, but it is for his feats on the cricket field that he is best remembered. His style was founded in baseball, which he played in his younger days, and when he toured England with the Philadelphians in 1897, 1903 and 1908 he found rich pickings among bewildered English batsmen who could not fathom how to play him. On his first tour he bowled Ranji first ball, and together in the three tours he took 252 wickets in first-class matches at an average of 16.22.

Once in a match against New York, King overheard one of his opponents boasting that he would smash his bowling all round the ground. When that batsman arrived at the crease, King ordered all the fielders back to the pavilion with the exception of deep fine-leg.

'I'll deal with this fellow myself,' he said.

'Oh,' said the batsman, who had not been totally unnerved, 'then why are you keeping fine-leg?'

'So he can field the ball after it has hit your wicket,' retorted King.

He prepared to bowl, holding the ball cupped baseball-style in both hands above his head just before he released it. The delivery was viciously fast, swerved heavily late in flight, moving from outside the off-stump to take the leg bail. The ball then soared straight into the hands of deep fine-leg.

DOGGONE FAST

Another early speed merchant was George Brown of Brighton, who was at his best in the early 19th century (he beat Squire George Osbaldeston, a great all-rounder, at single-wicket in 1818). In a practice match Brown bowled a ball which beat the batsman, wicketkeeper and longstop and headed straight for a dog beyond the boundary. The owner of the dog tried to stop the ball with his coat but it smashed through it and killed the dog.

SHORTEST SPELL IN TEST CRICKET

According to some newspaper reports, S. M. H. Kirmani's offering in the Fifth Test between India and West Indies in 1983 was not only brief but in a technical sense non-existent. With West Indies needing one run for victory the Indian wicketkeeper came on and bowled a no-ball. The moving finger in the scorebox was said to have dropped its pencil at that juncture and scratched its puzzled head. What to write? Did Kirmani bowl or didn't he?

It later emerged that Kirmani had delivered one legal ball before the no-ball, and so the scorers in fact had been less confused than the journalists.

ODDEST ACTION

Newspaper editors could not decide which species of reporter to send to watch Les Glennon bowl for Brightlington, the Yorkshire League side. Was he news, sport or features? On which page did you print a photo showing a right-arm medium-paced bowler who delivered every ball he bowled from behind his left ear? Written descriptions varied from the logical to the confused, and one reporter came away deciding he had just seen a 'right-handed left-arm seamer'.

Les apparently contributed little to the debate, content to let his action, and its effectiveness, be a reply in itself. His best figures were 7 for 14 in 17 overs, and in 1964 he averaged four wickets an innings through the season. It is therefore superfluous to reveal that in twenty years he bowled only one wide.

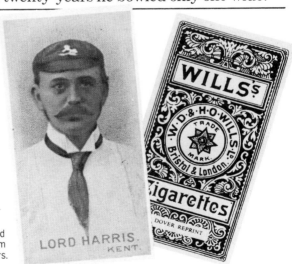

Lord Harris, who stood no nonsense from his bowlers.

LORD HARRIS. KENT.

WILLS'S
W. D. & H. O. WILLS
TRADE MARK
Bristol & London.
Cigarettes
DOVER REPRINT

MOST DISGRACEFUL DELIVERY

When 'Punter' Humphreys played in a trial at Tonbridge he bowled a no-ball and was immediately sent off by Lord Harris. Later his lordship explained: 'I did that for your own good, Humphreys. A fast bowler can be excused a no-ball occasionally, but not a slow bowler like you.'

DISASTERS
OF
DISMISSAL

To be dismissed is a disaster for every batsman. Even if he has already scored a century, there will always be commentators and spectators more than willing to say that he 'should never have got himself out like that'. Any dismissal through a defensive stroke is humiliating, no matter what the circumstances, for it is a concession of victory to the bowler and the opposition.

　　　　To counteract the public shaming of dismissal, many batsmen have contributed to the evolution of a set of popular phrases for explaining away their failures at the crease. As yet the wisdom of this collection has not been published, but each year it grows ever larger through oral transmission alone. Popular themes include diabolical umpiring, rotten pitch, misplaced sightscreen, dazzled by boy with mirror, verbal intimidation by wicketkeeper, and many many more.

Surprisingly, though, some batsmen do have **genuine reasons to feel aggrieved.**

    In a game played between two military sides in India in 1899, the fielders wore their helmets to protect them against the sun. One man rushed to catch a skier but lost track of it; the ball then plummeted down and lodged on the spike of his helmet. In Ceylon in 1898, in a match between the Combined Royal Artillery and a Royal Engineers XI, another fielder misjudged a skier and the ball crashed through his pith helmet. In both these instances the batsman was given out because neither helmet had been used deliberately.

Pith helmets in the sun – standard headgear for British cricketers in 19th-century India.

    During a match at Attleborough, Norfolk, a batsman shaped up to slash a ball through the slips. Second slip took evasive action and turned his back but the ball struck him in the back of the neck and dropped down inside his shirt. First slip retrieved the ball and was duly credited with the catch!

    Equally unfortunate was the batsman who was dismissed off the bowling of H. Leahy in a match against the London club Maurice C.C. He hit a lofted drive in the direction of long-off. The fielder, running in, misjudged the ball which hit him on the head and rebounded 15 yards to the bowler who completed a fine if fortuitous 'caught and bowled'.

    Not all batsmen dismissed in unusual ways can claim misfortune, and some indeed **bring disaster upon themselves.** In a regimental match at Simla in 1901 Captain Onslow had made 23 when he was beaten by three consecutive deliveries. This blow to his confidence and, more importantly, his pride led to a suitable expletive; at the same time the good captain stamped his foot. Unfortunately for him it was the only one behind the crease at the time, and as his foot left the ground the fast-thinking keeper, M. O'Tandy, whipped off the bails for an impressive stumping.

    Sarcasm was Peter George's downfall in a match between South

Woodford 2nd XI and Walthamstow 2nd XI in the mid 1960s. He was hit on the pads by three successive deliveries and each time loud optimistic appeals were turned down by the umpire. When a fourth and even wider ball hit him on the pads, Peter George got in first with his own sarcastic appeal. Up went the umpire's finger and the shame-faced batsman had to go.

Six words cost Barnsley's Ken Leather his wicket in a Yorkshire League match against Rotherham in 1980. When his partner's drive appeared to be going over deep mid-off's head, he shouted: 'Come on, Martin, it's safe.' For this he was given out obstructing the field, the umpire judging that his shout had distracted the potential catcher.

'Retired hurt' is a frequent occurrence and of course counts as an uncompleted innings. This was some consolation to Danish all-rounder Erik Madsen during a Forty Club match at Odense in 1976. The umpire, who also happened to be a doctor, had already given Madsen out caught behind when he noticed that the batsman was suffering some physical agony. Diagnosing that his arm had been broken well above the glove, the umpire reversed his decision and Madsen retired hurt.

The decision to retire is usually a batsman's own, although the reasons are often bizarre. Scorebooks in existence record J. Williams of the Dorset Rangers as having **'retired hot'** during a match at Carcavelos in Portugal in 1981, and J. Southerton of Surrey as 'retired thinking he was caught' in a match against M.C.C. and Ground at the Oval in 1870. Mr Southerton had skied the ball and set off immediately for the pavilion, partly in disgust at his poor shot and partly because he thought he was certain to be caught; when the chance was missed, he

Another national disaster, and a personal one for Australian batsman Woodfull, clean bowled by Larwood for a duck in the 1932–33 Ashes series.

refused to return – but in any case it is more than likely that he would have been run out.

Perhaps the most tragic retirement story, if it happened, is of the batsman who faced a tearaway fast bowler on a fiery pitch. The ball flew off the shoulder of the bat, struck the batsman a fearful crack on the temple and was caught by the wicket-keeper. His appeal was upheld but the batsman lay dead in his crease. After he had been carried off and the game abandoned, someone in the pavilion mentioned that the doctor had reported death as instantaneous. This sparked off an immediate cricketing debate. The batsman had obviously been dead before the catch was taken. Could he therefore be dismissed after his demise? The majority view was that the scorebook should be revised to read **'retired dead'**.

H. J. Heygate had not exactly got into his stride before he was given out in a match between Somerset and Sussex in 1919. Sussex lost their ninth 2nd innings wicket with the scores level but Heygate, their No 11, was sitting in the pavilion in his civvies. Crippled with lumbago he had earlier decided not to bat, but was sportingly invited by the Somerset secretary to go in to try for the winning run. He was helped on with his pads and, after taking off his waistcoat and watch chain, he proceeded slowly to the wicket. By the time he arrived, well over two minutes had elapsed. A Somerset fielder appealed and the umpire was forced to refuse Heygate his innings and send him painfully back to the pavilion. The match was declared a tie.

To hit one's own wicket is an exceptionally disastrous way to be dismissed, as well as being a gift to the bowler who never intended such an outcome. However, there must have been something about Tich Freeman's bowling which actually induced batsmen to hit their wicket. In 1921 in the match at Lord's between Middlesex and Kent, three of the first four in the Middlesex 1st innings were out 'hit wicket bowled Freeman'. What was more Patsy Hendren, the Middlesex No 4, and Freeman's third victim, had also been out hit wicket in the away match at Canterbury three weeks earlier. Since, at Lord's, he was dismissed during the first over he faced from Freeman, Hendren had therefore been induced to hit his wicket twice within the space of six deliveries.

The gods were assuredly with R. N. Burchnall in the Harrow v. Winchester match of 1965. He was struck on the head by a bouncer which knocked his cap off his head onto the wicket where it hung without dislodging a bail. Burchnall went on to make 141. Dick Horsfall of Essex was also fortunate to evade dismissal in a 1957 match with Glamorgan. He was hopelessly stranded when a fielder threw down the wicket at his end. But the observant umpire had seen the bails removed by a gust of wind a split second earlier, and quite correctly signalled not out.

M. P. Donnelly of Warwickshire had the distinction of being bowled by a ball which broke his wicket from the rear. In the match against Middlesex at Lord's in 1948 a ball from Jack Young hit Donnelly on the foot, bounced over his head, landed behind the wicket and spun back and removed the bails.

If there is a greater humiliation than being so obviously dismissed that no-one even bothers to appeal, it is being **out twice to the same ball.** This happened to Gilbert Parkhouse in England's 1st innings v. New Zealand at

Tich Freeman of Kent directing a Yorkshire batsman back on to his stumps.

Wellington on the 1950–51 tour. Facing Tom Burtt, he was given out l.b.w. but as the ball then trickled onto the stumps and dislodged a bail the umpires instructed the scorers to record the dismissal as 'bowled'. Andy Ducat was also doubly out in the Headingley Test of 1921 against Australia, his only Test appearance. A ball from fast bowler Ted McDonald broke his bat and a splinter fell on his wicket; at the same moment Jack Gregory took the catch at slip. The official verdict was 'caught Gregory bowled McDonald'.

Another batsman with little to complain about was H. Charlwood in a match for United South of England v. United North of England at the Oval in 1870. He played a ball into the air and set off for a run. The fielder dropped the chance so he turned for a second run. Reprieved, the fielder seized the ball, threw it in and Charlwood was easily run out at the wicketkeeper's end. At the same time the other umpire was signalling one short. Charlwood had failed to make his ground at either end.

THE MOST VIOLENT GAME

HOLD IT!

The recent introduction of the helmet has softened many a blow to cricketers' heads, but grievous bodily harm inflicted on the cricket field has never been limited to just one part of the body.

One of the most spectacular fielding accidents occurred in 1886 at Salisbury Plain, St Helena. *The Graphic* of 20 February reported that a fielder had chased a long hit so keenly that he **went over a cliff** and met his end on the rocks beneath. Just one year before, there had been a gruesome death on the

Somerset & Dorset railway line at Templecombe. A ball had gone out of play and been lost on the line. Joining the search, a youth named Tucker was crushed to death between two trucks which were being shunted, the railwaymen concerned having no idea that he was there.

C. G. Whittaker, playing for Kent in the middle of the 19th century, was more fortunate. Going to stop a fierce drive, he merely suffered the **loss of half his thumb.** Being a humorous man, and with a thrifty streak in him, he had the bone removed from the missing part and converted it into a pipe tamper.

From the batsman's point of view such mishaps can bring unexpected dividends. In August 1970 Chris Taylor, playing for the Lancashire club Moorside against Uppermill, struck the ball hard and high. A fielder dashed along the edge of the boundary to try and catch it but misjudged his charge. The ball **hit him on the head** and rebounded into the pavilion for a six; had the fielder missed it altogether, the batsman would only have got four.

A candidate for the most hard-done-by fielder must be the German novice who was recruited to make up the numbers in a pre-war Berlin League team. His captain, a Prussian of the old guard named Thamer, sent him to field at deep mid-off which Thamer reckoned would be the safest place while he himself opened the bowling with his off-breaks. Unfortunately, in his second over a skier came straight to the novice and he dropped it. Next over, the batsman played an identical shot and again the poor fielder could not hold the chance. His captain was so enraged by this double failure that he now marched across to deep mid-off and felled the player with a **right hook to the jaw.**

This story came to the ears of Major M. F. S. Jewell while he was leading the Gentlemen of Worcestershire on a tour of Germany in 1937, and during the farewell dinner he mentioned it to the German Sports Minister Von Tschammer und Osten, and suggested that such behaviour would not encourage young Germans to take up the game. The Minister replied that he had heard about the incident. 'But,' he added, 'I understand it was a *very simple* catch.'

Self-inflicted wounds are, it appears, a common category of cricketing injury. Eddie Hudson, batting for Exton Park in a Leicestershire League Cup-tie, **broke his leg** when he crashed into the stumps while hastening to avoid a run-out. He ignored his teammates' advice to retire hurt, and faced the next ball standing on his right leg with the left stuck out at a strange angle. From this odd stance he cover-drove a six to win the match in the final over.

'Batsman On Fire' could be the headline to many an incident in which players have proved beyond reasonable doubt that smoking can damage the health. The usual cause of sudden fireworks at the crease is that the batsman forgets about the box of Vestas in his trouser pocket, is then struck on the thigh by the ball and the box explodes. While the batsman prances about in agony, beating at his densely smoking trousers and possibly trying to wrench them off, the reactions of the onlookers – players and spectators – are usually remarkable for the lack of sympathy displayed. Spectators shout such unhelpful remarks as 'Lay the hoses on 'im', and wicketkeepers are inclined to think only of seizing the ball and stumping the victim as soon as he hops out of his ground. It is then often left to the humanity of the umpire to decide whether to give the man out or allow him to continue – provided he has the appetite to go on and has retained sufficient trousering not to offend the lady spectators.

Disabled cricketers share this robust attitude. More than a hundred years ago matches were common between **One-Arm teams and One-Leg teams.** The Greenwich Pensioners were particularly strong in both these divisions. In a match at Walworth in the 1840s, a batsman's wooden leg came off as he was running between the wickets. Relying on momentum and his good leg to get him to the far end, he hopped on. A One–Arm player fielding at point swooped on the wooden leg and used it to throw down the wicket. The umpire gave the batsman out!

Not a *danse macabre* but a mixed field of One–Arm and One–Leg cricketers.

A **fractured skull** was one of several extraordinary circumstances leading to a sequence of dismissals which is probably unique in the history of the game. The match was played in London over two Saturday afternoons, and at close of play on the first day the batting side had lost six wickets. On the following Saturday afternoon one of the not-out batsmen boarded a bus going to Kennington when he should have been heading for Kensington. He did not arrive at the ground in time to resume his innings and was ruled out by the umpire. One wicket had thus fallen without a ball being bowled.

Victim of the violent game.

FEBRUARY 26th, 1975
EWAN CHATFIELD "DIES" IN TEST MATCH

The heart of New Zealand cricketer EWAN
CHATFIELD stopped for three or four seconds after
he had been struck by a bouncer from the England
fast bowler Peter Lever, during the first test match
at Auckland.   Chatfield was given the kiss of life
and heart massage and taken to hospital, where he
was found to have a hairline fracture of the temple.

PHOTO SHOWS:-   Three pictures of the incident
as seen by television viewers on ITN's 'First
Report'.   Top picture shows Chatfield falling
after being struck by a ball from Lever; Middle
Picture, shows him receiving treatment, and
the bottom picture shows him recovering in
hospital.   H.Keystone   ML/869532

The first ball of the day was a no-ball which the batsman struck towards mid-on and set off for a run. The fielder stopped and returned the ball smartly and the batsman was run out. That made two wickets down on the day (eight in total) without a ball being bowled. The next ball was driven hard and straight, hitting the batsman's partner on the head, from which it rebounded and the striker was caught. Also en route for the pavilion was the non-striking batsman, who had suffered a fractured skull. Four men, effectively, were out and only one ball had been bowled. With nine wickets now down overall, the last man arrived at the crease but was ruled out as there was no-one left to bat with him.

Cricketing violence may erupt initially in the mind. In 1776 an Essex team due to play Kent at Tilbury Fort took strong exception to an unqualified player and refused to begin the game. A fight broke out and some of the Kent players ran into the guardhouse, got hold of a musket and **shot and killed one of the opposition.** An elderly invalid was run through with a bayonet and a sergeant was shot dead. Seeing that the pre-match exchanges were going against them, the Essex men took flight and escaped over a drawbridge. The Kent players then took to their boats and searched for them.

Not so long ago cricket in the Pacific used to be a very violent game indeed, and hair-raising incidents still occur. In a 1982 tournament in Western Samoa the batting side, Satupaitea, had their last pair at the wicket and needed one run to draw level. The batsmen went for a quick single and one of them was run out, giving their opponents, Solosolo, victory by one run. As the umpire, an international rugby forward named Ailso Leavasa, went to remove the stumps he was attacked by a member of the losing side and later died after being **hit over the head with a cricket bat.** Two men were arrested for this crime of passion and a third man vanished.

STRANGEST VENUES

The urge to play cricket is not lightly deterred by geographical obstacles or the distance of the chosen ground from Lord's. It was perhaps a little contrived of the twenty-two gentlemen who in 1800 staged their match **on horseback,** but some of the players probably felt more at home in the saddle anyway. Closer to the ground, **cricket on bicycles** has a wide popularity among schoolboys in the summer holidays, and **cricket on ice** has a history almost twice as long.

Midwinter cricket on ice at Sheffield Park, Sussex, home of the wealthy cricket benefactor the Earl of Sheffield. He footed the bill for Grace's team to go to Australia in 1891–92 and the Sheffield Shield series is named after him.

In 1838 a match was played on ice at Harewood, Yorkshire, against Stank. The home side scored 486, and the latter replied with 212 for 4. The high scoring suggests problems of mobility in the field, as does the feat of a batsman called Barrett who scored 13 with one hit. Quite why the match ended with Stank still in a position to catch their opponents' total is not recorded. Perhaps the ice melted; if so, the tactical lesson seems to be that on ice it is more rewarding to bat first.

Wisden records that 'All England will remember with a shiver and a shudder the long, sad and severe winter of 1878–79, commencing, as it did, in October and continuing into the middle of May; and even then the cold, nipping, bronchitis-creating winds seemed loath to leave the land they had so severely stricken.' But, continues Wisden, 'there is no black cloud without its silver lining, and one bright spot in this dark winter was that its severity enabled more cricket matches on the ice to be played . . .' We have not heard of cricket matches on ice recently but that year there were games recorded all over the country – at Hull, at Grimsby, at Eridge Castle in Kent, on a dam near Chesterfield, on a marsh near Gainsborough, on the Duke of Devonshire's pond at Swiss Cottage and on the Earl of Scarbrough's frozen lake.

Two games are perhaps especially worthy of recall. One was played by moonlight at Windsor Park. The local chronicle tells us that the moon was full and shone with 'truly splendid brightness throughout the evening and night'. There were several hundreds of spectators who apparently derived 'no end of amusement from the plight of players'. The totals were only 17 and 15 and the side that won by those two runs only had ten men.

One game that winter pitted Cambridge University against Cambridge Town – and in Cambridgeshire, as in most Fenland counties, there were some competent skaters around. So it is perhaps not surprising that the scores in this match were very high. In fact there was a rule in some Fenland matches that batsmen had to retire when they had made 25, and the result was often a tie with *everyone* making 25!

The surface at the Worcestershire county ground might have produced some interesting results in the 1889 season had not someone noticed in time that it had been sown in error with turnip seed.

Shipboard cricket was at its height in the days of the large cruise liners, and in fact 'deck cricket' is virtually a game in its own right. At first it was

played with a tethered ball, and then the ball was liberated and a coconut matting strip was laid with stumps set in a block of wood; the playing area – space permitting – was about 30ft by 60ft, and nets were rigged on spars to keep the ball in and to protect non-spectating passengers from being shelled while sunbathing or taking tea.

Under deck-cricket rules the officers of the P & O liner *Himalaya* were an unbeatable combination until 1969, defeating passenger teams which over the years included several Test players. In that year they lost the last and deciding match of a 'five test' series played en route from England to New Zealand. Venues for the five matches were, roughly, the Bay of Biscay, the Gulf of Guinea, the Indian Ocean, the Great Australian Bight and the Tasman Sea.

The frustrations of lost balls and the six-and-out rule were never tested aboard I. K. Brunel's *Great Eastern.* When this ocean-going mammoth – 680ft at the waterline and with a beam of 82ft 6in – was floating on exhibition before her maiden voyage in 1859, a grand cricket match was staged on her main deck. Reporters chronicling the event were much impressed that the ball never left the ship while play was in progress. One thing is certain: whatever the *Great Eastern*'s suitability as a cricket ground, she was by far the largest ship that any of

the newspapermen had ever seen, being almost exactly twice the length of the previous largest, and six times her tonnage. As a ship she had an unfortunate career, because she was too large to pay her way; perhaps she would have fared better as a kind of permanent floating Old Trafford.

Another venue of awesome dimensions was a **two-million gallon petrol tank** in Adelaide where a match was played in 1940. The metal playing area was over 100ft wide and was lit by electric bulbs. Runs were scored according to where the ball hit the side of the tank – a system that will be familiar to all back-garden cricketers.

Cricket in unusual venues can be brought to unexpected conclusions. A match on **Goodwin Sands** ended when the stumps were sucked under, and at the **South Pole** when John Reid, the former New Zealand captain, struck a six into the snow and the ball – the only one they had – vanished. That venue may in fact rank as the strangest of them all. The wicket was the Pole itself, which at the time (1969) was represented by a striped barber's-type pole with a

silvered reflecting glass ball on top. Another unique feature was that every shot played by the batsmen, no matter how they hit it, travelled north.

One of cricket's most famous pictures is a drawing by Captain Lyon, later turned into an engraving by Findon, of a game of cricket played in temperatures of 30° below zero inside the Arctic Circle between ships on Captain Parry's second voyage in search of the North-West Passage. Parry's journal of the voyage was published in 1824 with Findon's engraving as the frontispiece.

Just as polar cricket balls are drawn in a constant direction, so in the **United Arab Emirates** all heads respond uniformly to the call of the Muezzin, and turn to face Mecca. We are told that two postures are approved for cricketers interrupted in the course of a game: members of the fielding side should prostrate themselves in the usual way, but batsmen are permitted to remain standing with the head inclined in prayer and the hands placed reverently on the handle of the bat.

The Sheikh Abdul Rahman Bukhahir cricket ground in Sharjah, United Arab Emirates.

Roman Catholics at Downside School also stop playing the moment bells ring at six o'clock each evening. Many an opposing bowler has been confused in mid run-up to see a Downside batsman drop his bat and stand to attention. It is unclear whether dismissals should count if the batsman is bowled by a ball released fractionally before the bell sounds.

To any cricketer who has not been detained at Her Majesty's pleasure, the **prison field** must seem a strange venue. There are, of course, keen cricketers whose fate is continually to be detained in HM's lockups; to them, the prison field must seem the most natural venue on earth. In *College Harry*, the biography of an ex-convict, there is a description of a match played at Parkhurst, Isle of Wight, which posed an unusual moral problem. The opposing teams were a Habitual Criminals XI and the South of England Pickpockets. The Pickpockets batted first, but when one of the openers was given out by the umpire, himself a Habitual Criminal, the Pickpocket refused to walk saying that such a man could not be expected to give a reliable decision. It was an issue that needed delicate handling, and the Prison Governor was called on to adjudicate. The match was shortly resumed, and the Pickpockets won.

THEY
TRAVELLED
MOST
HOPEFULLY

One of the first cricket teams to travel long-distance – the England side bound for America in 1859.

In the 1870s Robert Louis Stevenson had many essays published in *The Cornhill Magazine*, a century before that name acquired its cricketing connection. In one, entitled *El Dorado*, he set down a dictum that has become a moral prop and justification for generations of failed cricketers. In full it reads: 'To travel hopefully is a better thing than to arrive, and the true success is to labour.'

One of the amateur game's **most hopeful travellers** must be Syd Levey, who perhaps experienced his worst (and therefore most truly successful?) moments on 4 July 1930. An Independence Day match had been arranged in Detroit between a home side and a Toronto XI. Both Toronto's opening bowlers grew overexcited on the eve of the match and were jailed in Detroit without the option until their case came up on the 5th. Two replacements were hastily summoned, Syd Levey and Ted Carlton, and they set off at 2 am from the capital of Ontario and arrived in Detroit about 9 am.

Detroit went in first and Levey opened the Toronto bowling. Next over, he fielded in the slips, and off the first ball dropped a catch and dislocated his finger. Detroit batted confidently, and eventually declared when their total comfortably exceeded 300; Levey's bowling figures were 0–108. Since both the replacement players had to be back in Toronto that night, they opened the batting. Carlton played the first ball into the covers, set off down the pitch and was run out by a direct hit. The batsmen had crossed, so Levey faced the next ball which was a shooter and bowled him. There being nothing further to detain them in Detroit, Carlton and Levey set off again for Toronto.

No **strikingly bad performance** can be achieved without persistence, either in the relatively short span of an over or longer ones extending over several matches or even the best part of a season. In the former category is the apocryphal feat celebrated in this limerick which was posted on the notice board of a village cricket club in the Twenties:

> 'There was a young cleric named Glover
> Who bowled 21 wides in one over
> Which had never been done
> By a clergyman's son
> On a Thursday, in August, at Dover.'

An over consisting of 27 balls is certainly a great labour, if not a record. This seems to have been set by J. H. Human in a match between M.C.C. and New Zealand at Dunedin during the M.C.C.'s 1935–36 tour. His great over was, moreover, a maiden. It consisted of 30 balls, of which six were good and produced no score, plus a larger mixed bag of 24 wides and no-balls.

In Sydney in 1926 it was the spectators who travelled hopefully, though we must spare some sympathy for the object of their attentions, the unfortunate W. H. Ponsford. Between October and December he had amassed 11 centuries in 11 matches. At the Sydney Cricket Ground posters went up which proclaimed: 'PONSFORD – Come to the Cricket Ground and see the **world's greatest batsman**.' Some 70,000 turned up to see the world's greatest batsman score 6 in the first innings and 2 in the second.

Another batsman who must have felt temporarily out of sorts was F. L. Morton. He batted No 5 when Victoria scored their record total of 1107 v.

W. H. Ponsford, who in 1926 was temporarily embarrassed by the slogan 'The World's Greatest Batsman'.

New South Wales at Melbourne in December 1926. The previous four batsmen hit 880 runs between them; Morton was run out for 0.

The record individual score for a batsman is not to be found in *Wisden*. It is the undefeated innings of 777 scored in 1919 by George Gunn, the famous and eccentric

George Gunn, of Notts, scorer of the largest individual total for a batsman – 777, which he amassed in a single-wicket challenge match.

Nottinghamshire batsman, in a single-wicket match. Gunn initially rejected the challenge by a local amateur of no great skill who wanted to play him for a stake of £100. But the amateur persisted, and Gunn eventually agreed to take part provided the stake was lowered to £5. The match began one evening on the Trent Bridge practice ground, and in $2\frac{1}{2}$ hours Gunn had scored exactly 300 runs. At the end of the second session he was 620 not out and his opponent, feeling no doubt that he had travelled far enough, invited Gunn to declare. He declined, but said he would allow the **toiling amateur** to bowl at a heavy roller six feet wide instead of at the stumps. The amateur agreed, but it made no difference to George Gunn. Halfway through the third evening he had increased his score to 777 when the amateur cracked. He threw the ball away and left Gunn to his triumph.

The rewards of success are not always easy to decipher. At Port of

Spain in 1948 the West Indian Andy Ganteaume and S. C. 'Billy' Griffith of England made remarkable Test débuts. Each opened for his country and Ganteaume scored 112 and Griffith 140. Both were dropped from the next Test, and although Griffith appeared on two further occasions for his country Ganteaume was **never picked again** and so retired with a Test average of 112.

It is conceivable that the bowler loaned to a Leinster XI for their 1968 tour was a cuckoo deliberately planted in their nest. His credentials were superficially adequate: the Leinster officials were told that he 'had played good-class cricket in England'. When the time came to test the new man's skills he turned in a bowling analysis that many in the Leinster side thought was fairly indifferent: 3 overs, 0 maidens, 74 runs, 0 wickets. Oh, and three lost balls.

Norman Harding, the Kent player, must have wondered whether the great journey of a career in county cricket was his true destiny. In 1937, on his first morning in the Kent 1st XI, he turned out for them at Dover against Gloucestershire and saw a hat-trick of catches dropped off his bowling by his new colleagues in the Kent slips.

Several other bowlers have registered **remarkable failures** in their efforts to nail a particular opponent. In 1926 the *Irish Times* reported that R. Bolton, playing for the Civil Service, clean-bowled C. P. Stuart of Clontarf with the first and third of three consecutive no-balls; the second ball was snicked to the slips, who missed it and the ball carried for four.

In 1884 a bowler called Glass, playing for Cheltenham College v. Royal Agricultural College, Cirencester, got the same batsman out three times in his first over with no-balls. Subsequently he neither took a wicket nor bowled another no-ball.

Almost a century later, in a championship decider played in August 1982, Dorchester bowler Paul Beer had Weymouth batsman Andrew Stone caught three times in the slips in the space of half an hour – off no-balls. Later Stone was dropped in the slips by a valid delivery from Beer, and went on to score 43 in a low-scoring match which brought his side the championship of the Dorset League.

The bowling career of E. J. Diver of Warwickshire followed a strange pattern which resisted all efforts at modification. In 1894, playing against Nottinghamshire at Trent Bridge, Diver's 6–58 proved an important element in Warwickshire's victory. **Further success eluded him absolutely:** in his remaining 116 first-class matches for the county he never took another wicket.

Two men with similar claims to the **most useless virtuoso performance** were Joseph Fowler and Stewart Purcell. In a Rotherham and District Works League match in July 1926, Fowler ran through the opposition taking 10 for 4. Needing 14 to win, his own side fared even worse and were all out for 11. Stewart Purcell, aged 15 at the time, could be forgiven for thinking he had done more than ease the way for his team, Old Galtonians of Harrow, when he bowled out the opposing side, Post Office ENTCH, with figures of 10 for 69. He had a rival, though, in ENTCH's Garry Turner, who took all 10 of Galtonians' wickets for 20 runs to bring victory for his side by 57 runs.

Teammates of Laurie Herbert may understandably have thought him 'bad ju-ju' (as they say in Yorkshire). In 1970 he was a member of the Smith's Sports side bowled out for a record low score of 7 in the Dales Council. Twelve years later he was at it again, playing for Oxford Place when they were dismissed for 7 by Ben Rhydding. If asked to defend his participation on two occasions in such a miserable feat, Herbert would be right to point out that the fault lay more with others than with him: for had he not been top scorer for Oxford Place with 2 not out?

There have not been many batsmen in England called S. S. Schultz. In our archive of bizarre cricketing feats, there is in fact only one S. S. Schultz, who not only played for England in the third-ever Test Match against Australia, in 1879, but who is also noted for scoring the **most pernickety double duck.** He was one of the Gentlemen of England XI who began a match against Oxford University on the Christ Church ground but then refused to continue batting on the bumpy pitch. The match was transferred to the Parks and restarted a few hours later. S. S. Schultz distinguished himself by being out first ball in both innings.

We pass now to **super-rabbits.** These are cricketers whom the arts of batsmanship have deserted, sometimes, it must seem, for ever. But for all their noughts and ones, they travel hopefully and some have even been known to break out again into glorious double figures.

Seymour Clarke's first-class career with Somerset was brief. It lasted for five matches and he was selected, it must be said, as a wicketkeeper. In those five matches he went to the wicket as a batsman on nine occasions and failed to score on any of them – though twice he was not out.

G. Deyes, playing for Yorkshire in 1907, suffered a bad patch of awe-inspiring dimensions. In 14 innings, his scores were 0, 0, 0*, 1, 1*, 0, 0, 0, 0, 1*, 0, 0, 0, 0 – a total of 3 runs. Things perked up later for him, and on his last three visits to the wicket as a batsman he scored 4, 1 and 12. At the end of the season his final average was 1.42.

W. E. Hollies, the great Warwickshire leg-spinner, was never selected for his batsmanship. All the same, even he must have felt he was plumbing the depths in 1948–50 when he batted in 71 innings without reaching double figures. Others approaching Hollies' bad run were E. W. Clark (Northants), who played 65 innings without a double-figure score, and Les Jackson (Derbyshire) who played 51 similarly barren innings. Overall champion, however, in this strange department may be J. C. Shaw, a left-arm bowler who in 109 innings for Nottinghamshire between 1865 and 1875 only once reached double figures.

W. E. Hollies, who failed to reach double figures in 71 consecutive innings.

CHURCHMAN'S CIGARETTES

CRICKETERS
A SERIES OF 50

19

E. HOLLIES
(*Warwickshire and England*)

In four seasons Eric Hollies has become one of the best slow leg-break bowlers in the country. He did little when first appearing for Warwickshire in 1932, but progressed so rapidly that in 1935 he took 130 wickets ,or less than 20 runs each and headed his county's averages. Touring the West Indies in 1934-35, he played in three Tests, taking seven wickets for 50 runs in the third encounter. A strained neck muscle compelled his withdrawal from the third Test against South Africa in 1935. Of slight build, Hollies is twenty-three years old.
A DOVER REPRINT

A. & A.C.CHURCHMAN

ED BY THE IMPERIAL TOBACCO CO.
GREAT BRITAIN & IRELAND, LTD.

E HOLLIES

Pity, now, the Harrow Constitutional team who in 1890 so successfully imitated poor Sisyphus. Labouring greatly against St Pancras United, they finally wrought a declaration from them at 209 for 1. But when they batted, the world crashed about their ears in the space of seven overs and they were dismissed without scoring a run.

Everyone at school loves the Staff match: the boys for the chances of revenge, the staff for the annual opportunity to assert that they can still do, as well as teach. The 1951 staff side at Downs Preparatory School near Bristol consisted of the headmaster, four assistant masters, the gardener, the rector and four fathers. Morale among the adults was high, and once it was established that they would bat first their agreed tactical plan was to knock up a brisk 70 or 80 and declare. 'Then the boys will have something to aim at.'

The Staff opening pair strode out to bat. Waiting for them were two determined bowlers aged 12 and 13, J. Smith and C. Whittington. The scoreboard charted the Staff's progress as follows: 0 for 1, 0 for 2, 0 for 3, 0 for 4, 0 for 5, 0 for 6, 0 for 7, 0 for 8, 1 for 9, 2 for 10. Unlike the Rotherham and District side mentioned earlier in this chapter, the Downs boys did not find this modest target beyond them.

BIZARRE FIELDING RECORDS

MOST SUCCESSFUL SUBSTITUTE

Until recently, substitutes were not meant to field in specialist positions even if they replaced specialist fielders. In 1928, in MCC's match against Queensland, Patsy Hendren was 12th man. Shortly after coming on the field as substitute, he took a brilliant catch in the slips. The Queensland captain suggested that perhaps Hendren should be moved out of the slips and he was duly placed at cover point, where he was soon in action again swooping on the ball for a spectacular run-out. Once again the opposition were unhappy and this time mid-off was agreed to be one of the least sensitive positions on the field. But Patsy Hendren was not to be denied: he held another fine catch in his new position and Queensland accepted their fate without further comment.

LARGEST HANDS

Pat Morfee, who played a few games for Kent between 1910 and 1912, has been credited with possessing the largest hands in first-class cricket. It is said that he could hold six cricket balls in one hand, though the records do not say whether Morfee's mitts were renowned for their safety.

FIERCEST THROWER-IN

Selection of a player as a specialist fielder is not uncommon although it is usually hoped that the player concerned may also be useful in a supporting role as batsman or bowler. In Fiji, however, the Nadi side had no illusions about the finer skills of Taito, who was in the side solely for his fielding and his ability to run someone out in almost every innings.

Invariably he fielded at short leg, where he was an impressive figure standing at 6ft 4in plus five inches of bristly hair. His method was to let a drive go past him until it was beyond the bowler's wicket and then he would chase it. He would quickly overtake it and then bend down on one knee and hurl the ball in with a spear-like motion, his right hand level with his shoulder for the entire follow-through. The ball travelled at immeasurable velocity and would never fail to take even a wary runner's wicket. His aim never erred and ball would crash into the stumps at the bowler's end, more often than not snapping one of them. No bowler ever attempted to catch or stop the return at the stumps, but kept well out of the line of the murderous trajectory. An opposing New Zealand Army batsman was doubly unfortunate when a ricochet off the stumps broke his jaw.

MOST CATCHES (IN THE FIELD) IN ONE INNINGS

F. Tait of Buller took eight catches in one innings during a minor representative match v. West Coast at Westport, New Zealand, on 15 December 1958. He took the catches in West Coast's second innings of 153, fielding at slip and mid-on off three different bowlers.

MOST CATCHES (IN THE FIELD) IN ONE MATCH

In a secondary school match played on 16 March 1974 in Wellington, New Zealand, Stephen Lane held 14 catches during the match. Thirteen-year-old Lane caught 7 opponents in each innings while playing for St Patrick's College, Silverstream v. St Bernard's College, Lower Hutt.

J. W. H. T. Douglas, at times driven by his fielders to understandable acts of impatience.

MOST FRUSTRATED CAPTAIN

Essex skipper J. W. H. T. Douglas found it hard to suffer setbacks with a smile. In a match at Weston-super-Mare, the last two Somerset batsmen had put on 143; in the process many chances had gone begging, mostly in the slips off Douglas's own bowling. Finally the slip-fielders botched one too many, and Douglas snapped. While the slips were still crouching, their heads turned in the direction of the departing ball, Douglas swiftly followed through and was soon tearing past his teammates, crying: 'All right, I'll fetch the bloody thing myself!'

MOST UNSUCCESSFUL IMITATOR

One veteran cricketer never ceased to talk about and imitate the exploits of his hero, Learie Constantine. For thirty years he practised Learie's method of picking up on the boundary and throwing the ball in through his legs. The result was always the same: the veteran fell over and the ball went for four. He also used to tell the youngsters at his club (any player under 50) how Learie bowled a slower ball, followed through like lightning, arrived just behind the ball and scooped it off the bat for a magnificent caught and bowled. The veteran tried out this strategem in a match, but the batsman spotted his very much slower ball and slammed it back down the pitch where the veteran, charging through head down, was instantly felled, all of three yards from the bowling crease.

Learie Constantine demonstrates a grip.

MOST UNDEREMPLOYED FIELDER

Many fielders complain that they do not have enough to do on the field, that they are left to freeze at third man or elsewhere in the deep, and in warmer weather cannot be blamed for dozing off. Most do get the occasional bit of work, however, even if they are not expecting it when it comes. One who almost escaped was Peter Smith of Essex. In a match between Essex and Yorkshire in 1935 he fielded through the two Yorkshire innings without touching the ball or being involved in any way until the very last ball – when fortunately he was still alert enough to catch Hedley Verity.

MOST DARING FIELDER

In more recent years the close-in fielding feats – catches, knockdowns, blood-on-the-grass, etc – achieved by Sid Barnes, Tony Lock and Brian Close have been widely admired. Many years before them, a celebrated champion at close-to-the-wicket fielding was E. M. Grace, brother of W. G. On one occasion he caught A. E. Stoddart, a renowned big-hitter, in a position which was so close to the bat that he was able to hand the ball on to the wicket keeper without moving his feet. E. M. Grace played for Gloucestershire for twenty-five years (1870–95) and is not known to have suffered any serious injury on the field.

DEADLIEST COVER POINT

The master in charge must have wrung his hands in horror – will they never learn?! In the match in 1962 between Wanstead County High School and George Monoux Grammar School, Walthamstow, there was a hat-trick of run-outs. Only one fielder was involved, Wanstead's Stephen C. Brooks who, fielding at cover, ran out three successive batsmen with three successive throws.

Stuff's cartoon of A. E. Stoddart, the big hitter, published in Vanity Fair.

MOST FLUSTERED FIELDER

Cricketers making their first appearance for a new team usually like to appear well-dressed so that even if their performance is not impressive, they do at least look as though they have played before. A cricketer making his début for the strangely named Leek Regex team cut an elegant figure in the field; new flannels, new buckskin boots, new cap. The batsman struck a skier into a swirling wind. As he swivelled uncertainly beneath, the fielder lost his cap, exposing a thick growth of black hair. A further gust of wind tore this from his head just as the ball descended. Snatching not quite simultaneously for ball and wig, he missed both and suffered the standard fine of 50p for a dropped catch and a more considerable blow to his dignity.

LUCKIEST FIELDER

In August 1973 William Goggin, aged 10, of Harrow, Middlesex, and his brother found £750 in £5 notes while retrieving their ball during a game of cricket on a piece of wasteland. The police could not identify the owners so the boys retained their find.

The right of the brothers Goggin to be rated 'the luckiest' was run close at Home Rule, a remote New South Wales township, where a fielder tripped over a pile of rubbish and came up holding a gold nugget, later valued at £8. The rubbish had been dumped from an abandoned mine. The cricket ground was immediately closed so that mining could be resumed. However, it is not known whether the fielder himself benefited from the new workings, or even whether he was allowed to keep the nugget.

LAZIEST FIELDER

The Leek Regex team also claim the laziest fielder and tell of how he met his fate (to see Leek Regex in action is probably the only way to judge the veracity of their claims). It is reported that during an away match a veteran of the Leek Regex side quickly became exhausted as the opposition kept hitting the ball over his head on a large ground on a hot day. What was more he was required to field at mid-wicket both ends. He always cycled to the match, so at the fall of the first wicket, 135 in $1\frac{1}{4}$ hours, he fetched his bike round to the boundary where he was fielding, and used it both to retrieve the sixes and to get into position for the next over. In the heat of the afternoon he was soon reduced to cycling more and more slowly across the square between overs, until finally the second ball of the new over was pulled fiercely round to short square-leg knocking him off his bike and smashing the front spokes. This also cost his side five runs for obstruction.

The youngest of the Grace
brothers, Fred, caught
Australian hitter Bonnor
off a skier so high that the
batsmen were well into
their third run when the
ball lodged in his hands.

53

ALL ENDS UP

It is bad enough to suffer defeat by an opposing XI; worse still when ten of the opposition might as well have stayed at home, so devastating was the all-round form of one player. At schoolboy level, the feat of David Gordon for Feltonfleet School must take some beating. In 1932, aged nine, he made 101 not out in Feltonfleet's score of 180–0. When the opposing side, Seabrook Lodge, batted, he took 9–35 and caught the other batsman.

In 1889 Dr M. E. Pavri, the captain of Parsis (who later appeared once for Middlesex) decided in advance that **teammates would be superfluous.** He single-handedly took on an eleven from Matheran, some seventy miles from Bombay, and scored 52 not out. It was agreed that the home side could not score from byes or leg-byes. Dr Pavri then dismissed them, without the help of fielders, for 38.

E. M. Grace once agreed to take a team to play a village XI not far from Thornbury, but only two of his players turned up. E. M. requisitioned eight spectators to make up the numbers, and he and C. J. Robinson put on 147 before E. M. was out; the rest of the team raised the total to 156 all out. Then E. M.'s team bowled out the home side twice, E. M. taking 14 wickets.

Paul Stanyard, the 1980 captain of Leeds League side Carlton, showed an acute understanding of what motivates certain fast bowlers. Before play began against Leeds Police, he told Malcolm Baddeley and Mel Tasker, who usually batted Nos 10 and 11, that they could open the innings if they first bowled out the Police for less than 30. Seizing the day, they dismissed their opponents for 29 and then showed beyond all reasonable doubt that they were **secret batsmen,** knocking off the required runs in 26 balls.

In 1939 Aberdeenshire's **most deadly weapon** was Alma Hunt, their Bermudan professional. In what turned out to be their last county match before World War II, Aberdeenshire visited West Lothian at the Boghall ground. West Lothian were dismissed for 48, Hunt taking 7 for 11. He then opened the batting and scored every one of the runs required; his two sixes, eight fours and five singles took him 25 minutes. Such domination by League pros is not altogether unusual but for the most part they allow the local players to gather some runs and wickets.

Readers will scarcely have forgotten that in 1983 the home season had one of its wettest starts for many a year. It is worth emphasizing the words 'one of', for in Britain we quite often have bad spells of weather, and in Manchester they have them all the time. So, although 1983 deserves to rank as a disaster, so do 1923 and 1924; 1930 and 1931 had their grim moments, and there were universal washouts in 1936, 1948 and 1950, to name just a few others.

Moreover, if rainfall in Britain is a relative matter, it is almost impossible to compare UK precipitation, and the disaster it brings, with what falls on other countries and to what effect. There is also a considerable danger of lapsing into the kind of competitive gloominess that only makes everyone involved feel worse. For example:

A Lancastrian: 'There's nowt to compare wi' 1979. Our side lost $81\frac{1}{2}$ hours of championship playing time in home games out of 221, and over $53\frac{1}{2}$ hours in away games. That's 30.58 per cent of playing time down't plugole. It were a miracle we finished 13th.'

A New Zealander: 'That's nothing. In 1982–83 our club season on the West Coast of South Island was meant to have started in October. Between then and 30th January we got one day's play. All the rest were totally washed out.'

Depression all round.

In this chapter we shall therefore confine our stories to the **genuinely spectacular.** A worthy candidate is the match played in July 1974 between Birmingham University and Manchester University at West Hills. After tea distant thunder was heard, and as C. D. Johnson faced up to the incoming bowler there was a blinding flash and a deafening bang and he was hurled to the ground. Everyone in the field fled to the pavilion, and from there looked out in awe at a great **circle of scorched turf** in the centre of the strip where the lightning had struck. No-one had been hurt, though all but two on the field had been knocked over. When the storm abated, the reluctance to return to the blackened pitch was universal, and the match was abandoned.

In 1981 night fell in Copenhagen before it was meant to. Six overs remained in a 30-overs women's league match between AB and Svanholm. Neither captain wished to abandon the match and the final overs were completed in the dark. The scorers were kept in touch by a relay of shouted messages from the centre; the umpires' role soon became fairly nominal as they had to rely on the players' honesty whenever there was an appeal – though l.b.w. decisions must have been impossible.

It was a windy day in the Simla Hills. The year was 1939. At Sanawar, the bowler was in his delivery stride when the matting beneath his feet sprang to life and flung him several feet in the air. Now the matting coiled itself and bounded across the field in fearsome leaps, enveloping the unfortunate fielder at long-on. Both he and the bowler had to be **stretchered off** for treatment. The cause of the incident? A miniature whirlwind.

Our earlier remarks about rain were not intended to devalue its destructive powers – particularly when it tumbles out of the sky for several weeks on end. At such times it can have spectacular side-effects on both cricket and cricketers.

The members of D. R. W. Silk's M.C.C. team which toured New Zealand in 1960–61 were greatly impressed by the journey between Nelson and Westport in South Island – a distance of some 90 miles – which took them seven hours. Intimations of disaster were offered when the last day of their match at Nelson was rained off. Some weeks earlier, heavy rain had washed out Sullivan's Bridge, on the usual route, and the players knew that they would have to be specially ferried – somehow – across the Buller River. Their coach was not far out of

Nelson before they encountered torrential rain which turned the roads into slippery tracks. At last they reached the river and slithered 150 yards on soggy clay to where the ferryboat waited.

It took an hour to transport the players plus three-quarters of a ton of baggage across the swollen river, three at a time. From the boat they loaded the baggage onto a trailer drawn by a tractor, while the players swarmed up a shingle bank to be conveyed half a mile by car to where a second coach waited. By this time they were both soaked and muddy and their suitcases were saturated.

Spectacular waterfalls cascaded beside the coach as it moved through the Buller Gorge, and the road was liberally snared with potholes and minor rockfalls. At one point everyone but the driver had to disembark before the coach was driven across a wooden bridge that seemed on the very **brink of collapse.** Then a much bigger rockfall, amounting to a landslide, fell just two hundred yards ahead of the coach. The players were offered the choice of getting out and wading through mud several inches deep, or staying put while Ministry of Works vehicles cleared the road. About half waded and half stayed in the coach. Those who took the soft option had a further **unscheduled thrill** when the coach, on its way through the path cut in the landslide, suddenly tilted sharply towards a 60-foot drop into the gorge below.

When the exhausted players reached Westport, the rain was still coming down heavily and there was no question of M.C.C. playing West Coast-Buller the following day. The match was abandoned without a ball being bowled. At the time the players would not have been consoled to learn that in 1876–77 Lillywhite's touring All-England XI had been stranded for two days at Otira, a tiny township a few miles further south. Those were stagecoach days and heavy rain prevented the horses from climbing the steep road over the Southern Alps. At least, though, Lillywhite's men had the comfort of a roof over their heads while they waited for the weather to clear.

'Incidents of the Drawn Match'. The Edwardian artist Ralph Cleaver selected as his main highlights of Birmingham's first-ever Test match the appalling weather which blighted proceedings to the last. This was the 1st Test of 1902, made notable when play was possible by J. T. Tyldesley's 138 out of 376, and by the skittling of the Australians for 36 (Rhodes 7 for 17).

BIZARRE BATTING RECORDS

MOST LOVESTRUCK INNINGS

A. J. Atfield, who played for Gloucestershire and Wiltshire, was married one morning in June 1903 at St George's, Hanover Square, then sped on the wings of love to Lord's where he exchanged his black outfit for a white one and struck a century before lunch in the Cross Arrows match.

MOST BASHFUL DÉBUTANT

During their lean spell in the early 1920s Worcestershire sometimes had difficulty in raising a full side. One day in the summer of 1921 Gilbert Ashton, headmaster of Abberley Prep School, received a phone call from the county captain, Maurice Jewell, who asked him to come and play that day against Essex. When he said that this was quite impossible, Jewell had an enterprising reply: he told Ashton to find someone else. In due course a junior member of staff at the prep school, A. M. Carr, was hijacked from his teaching duties and told to go and play for the county. Carr protested to his headmaster that he was no good, but Ashton had his orders. Carr played, and finished as top scorer for Worcestershire with 82.

ALL-TIME SMASH HITS

If, in search of all-time recordbreakers, we cast our net wider than the first-class game and delve into feats by school and club batsmen, there are rich pickings to be had. In place of Hanif Mohammad's record-breaking first-class score of 499, there is of course the one of 628 not out scored by A. E. J. Collins, aged 14, in a junior house match at Clifton College, Bristol. Collins carried his bat through an innings of 836 which lasted 6 hours 50 minutes spread over five afternoons.

For most runs in a season we have, instead of Denis Compton's 3,816, the 1980 aggregate of Brian Roe, the former Somerset opener, who collected 4,044 runs for Barnstaple Nondescripts. And for a record opening partnership, the highest to reach our notice is 641. This was scored by N. Rippon and T. Patton (who hit 408) on 19 March 1914 for Buffalo v. Whosonly at Gapsed, some 160 miles from Melbourne.

As for fast scoring, on 3 April 1969 Richard Edwards of Auckland showed why batsmen prefer eight-ball overs when he hit 62 runs in an over that included three no-balls. His scoring shots were nine sixes and two fours.

In 1932 John Goodman struck a purple patch on his way to making 256 for Australian club Blackheath v. Lithgow. In three eight-ball overs he scored 100 out of 102, including ten sixes and nine fours.

Credit for the fastest century may now go to Paul Pittioni, aged 13, who in March 1982, batting for St Patrick's Marist Brothers High School, Dundas, against Epping Y.M.C.A., passed the hundred mark in 16 minutes – more than twice the rate of Percy Fender's celebrated 100 in 35 minutes for Surrey v. Northants in 1920.

Arthur Edward Jeune Collins, the 14-year-old schoolboy wonder who in 1899 hit a record 628 not out for his house at Clifton College.

MOST DOGGED DUCK

Ivan Hutchings, at the age of 13, carried his bat through the innings for Sutton Under-13s v. Streatley. The exceptional feature of his innings was that while it lasted 26 overs his score remained 0 not out; his ten partners were dismissed for 32.

MOST EXHAUSTED BATSMAN

Batting for Hendon against Highgate School in 1879, T. A. Fison hit 264 not out in $3\frac{1}{2}$ hours, and ran every one of them. He then left the wicket and the scorebook records his departure as 'retired to catch train to Continent'.

Don Bradman returns to the pavilion at Headingley in 1930 after scoring 334, the highest Test innings up to that time. He was then aged 21, and he is still the youngest triple centurymaker in Test cricket.

CHAMPAGNE HITTING

Two colossi of the bat who need no introduction are the Graces, W. G. and E. M. In one of the more remarkable, and true, stories about W. G., the Doctor was leading the United South against the XXII of Grimsby. The Grimsby Worsley club, who were sponsoring the match, were worried that their team would not be good enough to last the full three days. As luck would have it a telegram arrived on the second day addressed to W. G. Grace. Since he was then batting, play was halted while the telegram was taken out to the wicket. From it W. G. learned that his wife had just given birth to a son, and he immediately ordered a longer halt in play while both teams took champagne with him.

After a while W. G. said: 'I would like to break a record to celebrate this,' and in honour of his wife battered the Grimsby bowling for 400 not out.

E. M. Grace, in his appearances for Thornbury, struck so many balls so hard and so far, many of them never to be seen again, that one umpire, the local postmaster, took to weighing down his coat pockets with up to nine spare balls. This worked well enough to preserve continuity of play until the day E. M. hit an earth-shaking double century and used up the postmaster's entire quota of spares.

'W.G.' – the golfer.

ONE BALL WAS ENOUGH

Victory after an innings lasting for one ball has occurred on at least three occasions. In 1913 St Dunstan's College, Catford 3rd XI dismissed their opponents for 1 wide, and their opening batsman made sure of victory by scoring two runs off the first ball he received.

Prep school Hordle House faced an altogether stiffer task by letting their opponents amass a total of 4. However, their opening batsman gave valiant chase and struck his first ball for six.

In the York Senior League in 1979 the Cawood players achieved a momentous win but may also have felt a sense of anti-climax in the way it came about. They dismissed Drinhouses for 2, then the first ball of their innings went for four byes.

Wilson Hartley pulled off what may be remembered as the ultimate humiliation of a bowler when he hit Walsden's Peter Green for six while playing for Rochdale in the Central Lancashire League. This was no ordinary six: it travelled an enormous distance and in a direction that many readers will find uncanny. The ball crossed into nearby Strines Street, smashed an upper window in one of the houses and came to rest on a bed – the bed of bowler Peter Green.

Six hit breaks the bowler's bedroom window

By Daily Mail Reporter

BOWLER Peter Green didn't only forfeit six runs when he sent down a 'soft one' to batsman Wilson Hartley.

Wilson gave it the treatment it deserved—and clouted the ball straight through Peter's bedroom window.

It sailed over the dumbstruck crowd at Walsden, Lancashire, cleared the fence and landed slap bang on the bowler's bed at his home in nearby Strines Street.

But minutes later Peter got his revenge. Wilson, batting for Rochdale in a Central Lancashire League game, attempted another windowbreaker and was caught on the boundary for 61.

Comeback

'The first one was an easy six, and I slammed it as hard as I could. But I hadn't the faintest idea it would finish up in his bed,' said Wilson, who was making a comeback after a spell in the 2nd XI.

'We'll be talking about this one for the next 20 years. The trouble is it couldn't have happened to a nicer fellow. Peter is a friend of mine. I wish I had done it to one of the other bowlers.'

Said Peter: 'I knew I bowled him a bad one. But I wish he had stayed in the second team.'

'I hope we are still friends,' said Wilson after hearing that the Walsden club's insurance covered the £2 bill for a new window pane in Peter's house.

After Peter's family fielded the stray six, and Peter took his revenge, Rochdale went on to 190 for nine, forcing a 'winning draw' according to League rules.

ODDEST SURVIVAL

In the 1983 final of the Oxford Inter-College Cricket Cup Balliol College won by scoring 243 and then bowling out New College for 165 – but without dismissing either opener. One retired hurt after top-edging a hook on to his nose and breaking it, and the other carried his bat for 58 not out.

BLOODTHIRSTY
CRICKET

Is cricket a gentle outing, a blameless afternoon in the sun, or is it a thinly veiled substitute for war? From the English shires come one or two indications that cricket and blood sports do indeed go hand in hand.

In Leicestershire the primeval desire to pursue foxes is echoed in the county cricket club's badge, which shows a lone example of *Vulpes vulpes* at the gallop, trying vainly to exit left from the circle in which the artist has trapped him. The county colours – scarlet and dark green – also have their blood-on-the-grass symbolism. Further proof of that county's love of the chase was surprisingly demonstrated at Lord's in 1972, on the occasion of the first Benson & Hedges Cup Final. As the Leicestershire players took the field Michael Farrin of the Quorn appeared in his pink coat on the team's balcony and sounded 'Gone Away'. This was presumably not intended to remind the county supporters present that their Illingworth-led idols were in the main a bunch of exiles, so much as to spur those players to victory. If so, it had its effect; Leicestershire took the trophy, and Yorkshire went home with their tails trimmed.

In that same year the rabbit population in a quiet corner of Somerset was badly shaken when the visiting cricketers in the next field turned out to be trigger-happy Gloucestershire gunmen. As the *Western Daily Press* reported the incident:

'The match at Compton House, Nether Compton, near Yeovil, was hardly cricket. It was The Players v. The Rabbits, and although the rabbits did most of the running, the odds were loaded against them.

'The match went smoothly enough until the visitors from Cowley, Gloucestershire, were half-way through their innings. Then shotgun blasts shattered the calm.

'A farmer was harvesting a nearby wheat field. And as the rabbits sped from cover, he took pot shots at them with his 12-bore.

'It was too much for umpire Peter Millard. He persuaded Compton club secretary Don Farley to take over at the wicket and slipped off to get his own gun and join the shoot.

'Unfortunately for the visitors, one of their batsmen, gamekeeper Colin Loving, was at the crease. He had just made a fine 50, when he realized he was in the wrong game. He was clean bowled next ball and dashed off to borrow the umpire's gun and catch his supper.

'Said Compton player Doug Jones: "The Gloucestershire lads haven't seen rabbits in their neck of the woods since myxomatosis. As soon as one of their players was out he stripped off his pads and joined the hunt."

'Mr Farley said last night: "The Cowley players who weren't batting seemed to produce shotguns from nowhere. They stood at the fence in their white flannels blazing away at the rabbits. There were about nine guns in use at one time."

'The final score was 20 rabbits bowled out – for keeps, and a two-wicket win for the home team.'

BIZARRE UMPIRING RECORDS

'How's that, Umpire?' From 'Humours of the Cricket Field', 1878.

LEAST LOGICAL UMPIRE

The feat of allowing one bowler to bowl consecutive overs is not unlike failing to count accurately to six, but also indicates a temporary breakdown in the logical processes. First bowler to get away with it was Australian captain Warwick Armstrong, who in a Test against England in 1921 completed the last over before rain interrupted play, then bowled the next one when play was resumed.

Alex Moir, the New Zealand spinner, achieved his 'double' in the Wellington Test against England in 1951. He bowled the last over before tea and the first after. A third man to bamboozle the umpires in this way was E. W. C. Vriens, playing for Holland v. Denmark in 1972.

In the Prudential World Cup in 1983 Viv Richards, playing for West Indies v. Zimbabwe at Worcester, returned to the wicket after a stoppage for bad light and took strike at the wrong end. He was out after two balls – but we wonder what would have happened had it had been a tight finish.

LEAST NEUTRAL

Nottinghamshire wicketkeeper Tom Oates was happy to become an umpire at the close of his playing career, but was not altogether acclimatized to the need for neutrality when, in one of his early matches, he was standing at the bowler's end and saw the batsman hit squarely on the pads. 'Owzat?' he shouted, filled with sudden excitement. 'Out,' said the bowler. And out it was.

MOST RETIRING

Industrial action hit the cricket field in June 1963 in a Birmingham League match between Smethwick and Walsall. Smethwick, the fielding side, unanimously voted not to accept a decision by one of the umpires and refused to continue with the match. The umpire appears to have accepted that he was not entirely blameless, since he then offered to retire from the game. This, as it turned out, suited Walsall very well. Currently bottom of the League, they went on to win their first match of the season by 9 wickets.

MOST ATTENUATED DECISION

In India the players can be even more contentious than in the Birmingham League. In a first-class match in Karachi, a batsman from Sind Province was at first relieved to survive an appeal for leg-before by the home side's bowler. He was less delighted when the bowler refused to accept the decision and, furthermore, insisted on telephoning his father for a verdict (his father just happened to be the executive in charge of the local cricket association). The call was put through and in turn the bowler, the batsman and the umpire spoke to the bowler's father, each giving his version of where the ball pitched, its line, and which part of the body it hit. After listening to all three men, the father gave the batsman out. When he had taken his pads off, that unhappy man vowed never to play cricket again.

MOST HEARTLESS DECISION

In a women's League match at Køge in Denmark the new batswoman was several months pregnant. On arriving at the crease, she asked the umpire for permission to bring on a runner. This was refused, on the grounds that her incapacity had not occurred during the course of the match.

Defenders of the Stumps – the umpires at Sydney in 1963 learn their new role in the dawning of the Age of Crowd Hysteria. Swarms of schoolboys invaded the pitch before the Australians had made the winning hit against England, and at the far end even managed to uproot the stumps

By 1974 Australian umpires were giving as good as they got when intruders ventured on the square. In this incident during the Melbourne Test v. England the errant spectator receives a timely clip round the ear.

LEAST NUMERATE UMPIRE

If a competition were held to find the umpire most likely to forget how many balls had been bowled in an over, four men would merit serious attention. Each is on record has having allowed an 11-ball over.

G. H. Pinney was the unfortunate victim on one of these occasions. Batting for Dorset Rangers v. Dorset Regiment, he was pleased to keep out five hostile deliveries from R. G. Shore and even more pleased to score a boundary off the sixth. Some of his pleasure evaporated when he observed Shore running in to deliver a seventh ball. This unnerving experience was repeated, and repeated. By the 11th ball, by which time the scorers were desperate for space in their books for another dot, Pinney was a demoralized man and his wicket was duly shattered. It later turned out that, when signalling the boundary, the umpire had taken the first five coins out of his pocket – and round they went again.

Phil Meech of Birstall managed to squeeze an 11-ball over past the umpires in a Central Yorkshire League match against Hanging Heaton. The sixth ball was again the decisive one. It was lost in a garden, and this was enough to throw the umpire's abacus into confusion. Sportingly – or is this an example of Yorkshire humour? – the opposing batsman said nothing but made no attempt to score off the next five deliveries.

Similar aberrations are known at county and schoolboy level. When J. M. A. Marshall was making his first-class début for Warwickshire against Worcestershire in 1946, he took a wicket with his sixth ball and collected an unwitting bonus of five more deliveries. At Wellington College one hot afternoon sanity was restored to the scorebook only by the intervention of one of the scorers – who happened to be the son of the offending umpire. Again, eleven balls had been bowled. By way of a supplementary explanation we are told that, in addition to the heat, it had been necessary to celebrate 'something or other' at lunch, and port had been passed round.

LEAST OBLIGING

When the last over was called in a Yorkshire Council match at Bramall Lane in the 1930s, Sheffield Collegiate needed one run to beat their great rivals Sheffield United. A batsman was run out off the first delivery and the umpires declared that the available playing time had run out. With the decisiveness of medieval tax collectors, they pulled up the stumps and walked off. Back in the dressing-room, Collegiate fielded their most fluent diplomats, who eventually persuaded United that the only honourable course was to go out and finish the over. They took the field, and with one more ball the match was completed. The umpires, needless to say, put on faces of stone and remained in the pavilion.

MOST GARBLED CALL

In a letter to *The Times* in 1935, Mr Charles Ponsonby wrote: 'I was playing in a match last year, and as a bowler delivered the ball the umpire ejaculated "B-r-r-r-r-" and, after a pause, added: "I beg your pardon. I meant to say 'no-ball', but I dropped my teeth".'

MOST ASSIDUOUS

It would be hard to find more caring umpires than the two who officiated at the Tadcaster Carnival Cup semi-final in 1980. They must also be considered as serious claimants to the record for making the latest light inspection. At 9.30 p.m. Thorp Arch needed eight runs off 11 balls to beat Shadwell. Rain then intervened, but had cleared by 9.45 p.m. The umpires, not wishing to be rushed, decided to inspect the pitch at 10 o'clock. By the time they reached the centre they needed no light meter to tell them that darkness had fallen; further play was ruled out.

Unlikely umpires: Surrey's celebrated pair Herbert Strudwick and Jack Hobbs put on white coats for a match at the Oval in 1946.

MOST UNCRICKET-LIKE PERFORMANCES

That infamous cliché 'It's not cricket' might never have got off the ground but for the feudalism of 19th-century Southerners, who believed that cricket must be a gentlemanly activity. In the Midlands and the North few men fell under this misapprehension, hence our examples of 'uncricket' are drawn entirely from the rugged lands beyond Leighton Buzzard.

A batsman in a Lancashire League match suffered a violent blow on the elbow from a bumper, dropped his bat and shrank to the ground while the ball lobbed into slip's hands. The stricken batsman's partner came down the wicket to offer help, and slip threw the ball back to the bowler.

'Quick,' hissed mid-off, miming to the bowler that he must run out the non-striker without delay.

The bowler, however, must have had Southern blood in him and refused to fall in with this unsporting plan. When mid-off ran over to try and tear the ball from his hand, the bowler put it in his pocket and walked away.

The stricken batsman then recovered enough to think about getting back to safety. Since he had virtually crossed with his partner he opted to head for the bowler's end and so add a single to his score. He sidled down the pitch, staggering once in a while to create the impression that he did not know where he was, then made a sudden dive for the crease, running his bat in just before mid-off, who had shamelessly winkled the ball out of his teammate's pocket, broke the wicket.

The air was rent with loud appeals. Mid-off appealed for a run-out, the batsman appealed for a run, and slip appealed for a catch. All were disallowed.

Too much backing-up can be guaranteed to sharpen the atmosphere if the match is tightly fought, or between traditional enemies. In Edinburgh, Heriot's F.P. and Watsonians do not give quarter and would not think of asking for it. In a 1982 encounter Watsonians were within 20 runs of victory, with three wickets in hand, when the bowler ran out the non-striking batsman for backing up too far. As if to make his point, he immediately ran out the next batsman in the same way. Now the scorers were in a quandary: how should they record the fall of two wickets without a ball being bowled?

It was not Watsonians' day. Their last batsman was also run out, though in a conventional manner.

The **lust for points** has turned many a cricketer's head. In a 1928 Minor Counties match between Leicestershire 2nd XI and Staffordshire, the latter made no effort to secure an easy first-innings lead since this would spoil their overall Championship percentage. Leicestershire captain G. B. F. Rudd then embarked on an over which yielded 14 wides and 47 byes, impelling Staffordshire to accept the lead – and a worse position in the county table.

With one ball to go in a Leeds League 2nd XI match in 1976, Colton were 124–9 in reply to Kirkstall's 124–7 declared. Colton's last man decided he was unlikely to score off the last ball and instead he sacrificed his wicket. This earned his team $2\frac{1}{2}$ points for the tie, which was one point better than they would have got had he defended his wicket and secured a draw.

In a Central Yorkshire League match in 1979, Batley and Gomersal **pulled out all the stops.** After an interruption for rain Gomersal had scored 141–5 but had only 100 minutes to bowl out their opponents, which seemed beyond

The LAWS of the NOBLE GAME of CRICKET.
as revised by the Club at St. Mary-le-bone.

THE BALL must weigh not lefs than Five Ounces and a Half, nor more than Five Ounces and Three Quarters. At the beginning of each Innings either party may call for a New Ball.

THE BAT

Must not exceed Four Inches and One Quarter, in the widest part.

THE STUMPS

Must be Twenty-four Inches out of the ground, the BAILS Seven Inches in length.

THE BOWLING CREASE

Must be in a line with the Stumps, three Feet in length, with a Return Crease.

THE POPPING CREASE

Must be Three Feet Ten Inches from the Wicket, and parallel to it.

THE WICKETS

Must be oppofite to each other, at the diftance of Twenty-two yards.

THE PARTY WHICH GOES FROM HOME

Shall have the choice of the Innings, and the pitching of the Wickets, which shall be pitched within Thirty Yards of a center fixed by the Adverfaries.

When the Parties meet at a Third Place, the Bowlers shall tofs up for the pitching of the Wickets, and the choice for going in.

It shall not be lawful for either party during a Match, without the content of the other, to alter the Ground, by rolling, watering, covering, mowing, or beating. This rule is not meant to prevent the Striker from beating the ground with his Bat near where he ftands during the Innings, or to prevent the Bowler from filling up holes, watering his ground, or using fawdut, &c. when the ground is wet.

THE BOWLER

Shall deliver the Ball with one foot behind the Bowling Crease, and within the Return Crease, and shall bowl four Balls before he changes Wickets, which he shall do but once in the fame Innings.

He may order the Striker at his Wicket, to stand on which side of it he pleafes.

THE STRIKER IS OUT

If the Ball is bowled off, or the Stump bowled out of the ground.

Or, if the Ball, from a ftroke over or under the Bat, or upon his hand, (but not wrifts) is held before it touches the ground, although it be hugged to the body of the Catcher.

Or, if in ftriking, or at any other time while the Ball is in play, both his feet are over the Popping Creafe and his Wicket put down, except his Bat is grounded within it.

Or, if in ftriking at the ball he hits down his Wicket.

Or, if under pretence of running a Notch, or otherwise, either of the Strikers prevent a Ball from being caught, the Striker of the Ball is out.

Or, if the Ball is ftruck up, and he wilfully ftrikes it again.

Or, if in running a Notch the Wicket is ftruck down by a throw, or with the Ball in Hand, before his Foot Hand or Bat is grounded over the Popping Creafe. But if the Ball is off, the Stump muft be ftruck out of the ground.

Or, if the Striker touches or takes up the Ball while in play, unlefs at the requeft of the other Party.

If with his foot or leg he ftops the Ball, which the Bowler in the opinion of the Umpire at the Bowler's Wicket fhall have pitched in a ftraight line to the Wicket, and would have hit it.

If the Players have crossed each other, he that runs for the Wicket which is put down, is out; if they are not crofsed, he that has left the Wicket which is put down, is out.

When a Ball is caught, no Notch to be reckoned.

When a Striker is run out, the Notch they were running for is not to be reckoned.

If fo Balls call'd, the Striker fhall be allowed four, but if more than four are run before loft Ball is call'd, then the Striker to have all they have run.

When the Ball has been in the Bowler's or Wicket-keeper's hands, it is considered as no longer in play; and the Strikers need not keep within their ground till the Umpire has called Play, but if the player goes out of his ground with an intent to run before the ball is delivered, the Bowler may put him out.

If the Striker is hurt, he may retire from his Wicket, and have his Innings at any time in that Innings.

If a Striker is hurt, some other Perfon may be allowed to ftand out for him, but not go in.

If any Perfon stops the Ball with his Hat, the Ball is to be confidered as dead, and the oppofite Party to add Five Notches to their Score; if any are run, they are to have five in all.

If the Ball is struck up, the Striker may guard his Wicket either with his Bat or his Body.

In single Wicket Matches, if the Striker moves out of his ground to strike at the Ball, he shall be allowed no Notch for fuch ftroke.

THE WICKET KEEPERS

Shall stand at a reafonable diftance behind the Wicket, and fhall not move till the Ball is out of the Bowler's hand, and fhall not by any noife incommode the Striker; and if his hands, knees, feet, or head, be over, or before the Wicket, though the Ball hit it, it fhall not be out.

THE UMPIRES

Are the sole judges of fair and unfair play, and all difputes fhall be determined by them; each at his own Wicket; but in cafe of a Catch, which the Umpire at the Wicket cannot fee fufficiently to decide upon, he may apply to the other Umpire, whofe opinion is conclusive.

They shall allow Two Minutes for each man to come in, and Fifteen Minutes between each Innings; when the Umpire fhall call Play, the party refusing to Play fhall lofe the Match.

They are not to order a player out, unless appealed to by the Adverfaries.

But if the Bowler's foot is not behind the Bowling Creafe, and within the return Creafe, when he delivers the Ball, they muft, unasked, call No Ball.

If the Striker runs a fhort Notch, the Umpire muft call No Notch.

The Umpire of the Bowler's Wicket, fhall be first applied to decide on all Catches.

The Umpires are not to be changed during the Match, but by the consent of both Parties.

BETS.

If the Notches of one Player are laid against another, the Bets depend on the First Inning, unless otherwife fpecified.

If the Bets are made upon both Innings, and one Party beats the other in one ining, the Notches in the First Inning fhall determine the Bet.

But if the other Party goes in a fecond time, then the Bet must be determined by the number on the Score.

Published by John Wallis, 13, Warwick-Square, London.

them. However, if they could bowl their full allocation of 43 overs they stood to earn a 4–1 winning draw, rather than sharing the points 2–2. The general view was that they should go for the 43 overs.

They soon found that precious time was wasted each time a Batley wicket fell. Instructions were given that catches were to be dropped. Batley's batsmen responded by trying to get themselves run out. Gomersal came back by throwing the ball over the boundary; this conceded 4 runs but made the ball dead. Then the Batley captain deliberately hit his wicket, only to be defeated in his ploy by Gomersal's fielders, who did not appeal and so the umpire could not give him out.

All this politicking and manoeuvring took up so much time that the 100 minutes elapsed long before 43 overs could be bowled and the teams ended with a 2–2 draw – until they were reported to the League. The League severely reprimanded both captains, fined the clubs £5 each and deducted their points.

BIZARRE
WICKETKEEPING
RECORDS

MOST ALL-ROUND PERFORMERS

It is not so surprising that some wicketkeepers nurture bowling dreams. If you think of all the hours they spend crouched in bulky pads, hands trapped in those massive sweaty shovels, looking down the pitch with a near-ideal view of each bowler's action and performance ... then you can see that there must be days, with the score at about 303–2, when the wicketkeeper is forced to conclude that he could hardly do worse than some of his idiot colleagues. Besides, he is the only one who has *really seen* what has been going on.

Two veteran 'keepers who conspired to bring reality into their dreamworld were Arthur McIntyre of Surrey and Leslie Compton of Middlesex. When the two counties met at the Oval in 1947, both wicketkeepers wangled themselves a bowl – the only occasion in first-class county cricket when both wicketkeepers bowled and batted in addition to their usual duties.

The England wicketkeeper Alfred Lyttelton took 4 for 19 against Australia in the Oval Test of 1884, and another England wicketkeeper, A. C. Smith of Warwickshire, frequently bowled with success for his county.

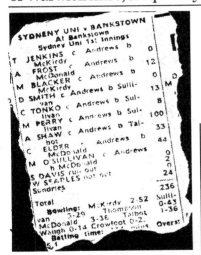

MOST VICTIMS IN AN INNINGS

In November 1982, playing in a first-grade match in Sydney for Bankstown, the suburb which produced Jeff Thomson and Len Pascoe, wicketkeeper Les Andrews caught the first nine Sydney University batsmen. Only their No 10 escaped the 'keeper's gloves–and he was run out at the bowler's end.

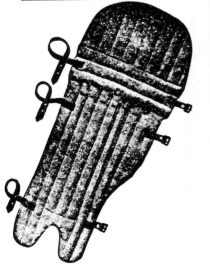

A safe pair of hands.

HAT-TRICK OF STUMPINGS

Playing for Gloucestershire v. Somerset in 1893, W. H. Brain stumped three opponents off successive balls from C. L. Townsend, who was then 17 and still at school, so something of an unknown quantity on the county circuit. Brain's achievement is the only incidence of a stumping hat-trick in the first-class game.

WICKETKEEPER WITH TWO HATS

In the Somerset v. Oxford University match in 1901, the Oxford wicketkeeper was injured and the captains agreed that Somerset's Rev. A. P. Wickham should keep wicket for both sides.

BEST BEGINNER

New Zealand's outstanding left-handed batsman in
the years after World War II, Bert Sutcliffe also made
a recordbreaking début as a wicketkeeper. In a match
against Central Districts at Napier in 1951–52, Otago's
regular 'keeper had to withdraw because of a family
bereavement. Sutcliffe took over behind the stumps,
held four catches in Central's first innings and
conceded no byes in totals of 399 and 74–1.

BREAKS IN PLAY

All interruptions, whether for drinks, lunch or tea, or for some more singular reason, carry with them the common potential for disaster: the players' rhythm is broken, adrenalin may cease to flow, backs stiffen, and, on resumption of play, they may well find that something is crucially altered. Unscheduled breaks in play offer the greatest scope for disaster. Examples are:

Earthquakes. Mohinder Amarnath of India was running up to bowl to Viv Richards in a 1983 one-day international at Queen's Park Oval, Trinidad when a strong tremor shook the entire ground, stopping play for five minutes. Damage to players was minimal, apart from the shock to their concentration, but several spectators in the 30,000 crowd were injured through leaping out of stands which they thought were about to collapse.

Dazzle. David Sheppard and Ken Barrington were batting late in the day during the Third Test between England and New Zealand at Lancaster Park, Christchurch in 1963. The evening sunshine, reflected off the aluminium front of a new grandstand roof, bounced suddenly into the eyes of the batsman, wicketkeeper and fielders behind the stumps at the striker's end. There was no possibility of continuing, and play was halted ten minutes early.

Trains and boats and planes. The Erinoid ground at Stroud, used by Gloucestershire between 1956 and 1963, was situated in the angle of the railway lines to Stroud and Nailsworth. On one occasion a locomotive had stopped behind the bowler's arm and the batsman was sufficiently put off that he waved to the driver to move. Unfortunately the driver felt that the signals of his employers were more important, and refused to advance until the essential arm was raised, letting him through.

Batsmen visiting Pottington Field, Barnstaple, were occasionally surprised to find their attention drawn away from the bowler by large ships creeping across behind the umpire's back. This form of interruption caused nothing like the consternation aroused on the day that a batsman at another ground looked up to find not only the bowler advancing towards him but, just to his right and about thirty feet up, a biplane with jets of coloured smoke pouring behind it. Everyone on the field flung himself to the ground until the danger had passed. Play was resumed for one ball, and then the biplane came round again, this time flying upside down with the pilot hanging out of it like

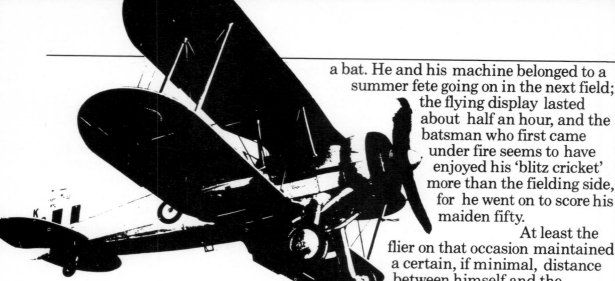

a bat. He and his machine belonged to a summer fete going on in the next field; the flying display lasted about half an hour, and the batsman who first came under fire seems to have enjoyed his 'blitz cricket' more than the fielding side, for he went on to score his maiden fifty.

At least the flier on that occasion maintained a certain, if minimal, distance between himself and the cricketers, unlike the surprise visitors to the match in 1974 at Trent Bridge between Nottinghamshire and the Indian touring side – two amateur parachutists who had strayed off-course and came down in the centre of the field of play, narrowly missing the wickets.

Birdmen alighting unexpectedly on cricket fields tend at least to survive, which is often not the fate of **real birds.** One of the best-known Last

In fond memory – the bird and the ball that killed it, now preserved at Lord's.

Flights is that of the Lord's sparrow which in 1936 was struck and killed by a ball bowled by Jehangir Khan to T. N. Pearce. In 1896 a Surrey Colts batsman called Higgins knocked a sparrow into the next world with an off-drive at the Oval. Swallows have been bowled out on various occasions, both in England and Australia. A happier variant is the story of the Dublin swift.

During a match at St Stephen's Preparatory School the batsman played his stroke, the slip fielder stuck out his hands and caught a low-flying swift. The boy was so taken aback by this extraordinary accident that he was there and then violently sick. The bird, on the other hand, quickly perked up after its release and flew away, apparently little the worse for being caught in the slips. The question remains whether the boy was sick because of the swift or the dropped catch.

Magpies are renowned kleptomaniacs and it would not be surprising to find a clutch of stories relating to magpies and stolen cricket gear, even though the ball may be too big for the beak. Quite what the magpie was up to one day in Cheshire, no-one could decide. Every time the bowler came in to bowl, the magpie ran on to the pitch and stood in front of the stumps. This went on for four or five overs, and the bird only flew away when the club bar was opened. It then perched on the roof of the building, and took no further part in the game.

In Trincomalee, Sri Lanka, an umpire had a narrow escape when a **two-foot-long fish** plummeted out of the sky and landed at his feet. No flying fish this, simply the dropped catch of a sea eagle which had been harassed in the air above the cricket ground by a flock of crows.

That fish was done for, we may assume, long before it reached the cricket field. But pity the unfortunate grayling which was swimming along the River Yorke one afternoon in 1934, decided to rise and was instantly struck and killed by a cricket ball hit into the river by S. Rayne in a match between Hawes and Aysgarth. The fielder stepped into the river and retrieved both ball and fish, which, for the record, measured $10\frac{1}{2}$ inches.

In the Indian sub-continent cricketers do well to stay on their toes and keep half an eye out for **snakes,** which are on record as having brought several playing careers to an abrupt end. Another danger is from **attack by buffalo,** which think nothing of invading cricket pitches. Closer to home, the British bull is a mean opponent when it charges onfield without warning. When a bull burst in on a local match at Dover in 1892 the players scattered in all directions, then watched in terror and amazement while the bull thundered up to the wickets and tossed them out of the ground.

By virtue of their size, cricketers prefer to deal with smaller mammals such as the rat, the stoat and weasel, which sometimes offer amusing diversions from the main business of the day. The *Athletic News* in June 1895 reported a fine contest between Mr Roper, a visiting Liverpool batsman, and a **Darlington weasel.** This weasel had earlier dashed on to the pitch with four companions, then was isolated from them by Mr Roper who charged at it waving his bat with murderous intent. The weasel neatly avoided the swings of the Liverpool man and crowned an impressive display of evasive running by going to ground in a hole on the banks of the River Skerne which ran alongside the ground.

Less fortunate were the **rat at Loretto,** fatally struck by a cricket ball as it emerged from its hole on the boundary, and the **stoat** which, in the same year, 1885, attempted to cross the wicket during a match at Royston. One of the fielding side responded to the intrusion by wrenching out a stump and hurling it at the stoat. It was a handsome throw, by all accounts, but very tough, surely, on the stoat which was speared and instantly dispatched.

The **animal world struck back** five years later. The Adelaide Oval was the venue selected; the match was between Members of Parliament and The Press. At the start of play all was calm, but by mid-afternoon the air was so thick with locusts that the fielders could barely see the ball and few of the spectators who stayed had any idea what was happening out on the pitch.

For two hundred thousand locusts substitute one telephone call: the effect was almost as disruptive. At Howick, near Pietermaritzburg, in 1958 play was suddenly interrupted when one of the batsmen had to go off the field to take an urgent call from his wife. Fearing bad news, he took the receiver with some trepidation and heard the voice of his beloved demanding to know where he had put the soap!

In matters of detail, few people are more astute than Yorkshiremen, and it is hardly surprising that it should have taken that eminent Yorkshireman

Cricket stumped by hot air balloon

By Mary Ackroyd

OWZAT! The visitors' seventh wicket stand collapsed sensationally on the village cricket pitch at Curdridge yesterday. In fact, pretty near everything collapsed.

Both sets of stumps fell down simultaneously. The batsmen were bowled completely over. The bowler fell flat on his face.

The entire Curdridge XI were skittled out where they stood in the field. And all the villagers collapsed — in laughter.

"It was the funniest thing you've ever seen in your life," said eyewitness Mr. John Adams.

Half-an-hour before "ballon stopped play" was recorded by the village cricket scorer, the huge grey and white hot air balloon advertising the Southampton opening of a new burger restaurant had lifted off gracefully from the city's Palmerston Park.

"We intended to fire on for about an hour, drifting peacefully over the Hampshire countryside, before coming down in a suitable field in the Wickham area,'' explained apologetic pilot Tony Bolger, of Calmore Road, Calmore.

"But unfortunately the heat of the day used up a lot of our fuel and we were forced to come down rather early. The choice, when it came, was either Curdridge cricket field or a nearby wood.

"We chose the cricket field because it was far safer and we knew that everyone there would see us coming and have time to get out of the way . . .''

Virtually everyone in Curdridge did see the balloon coming and gazed skywards, open-mouthed in astonishment as the great billowing sphere drifted gracefully to earth.

But only at the last minute was it realise the landing would com slap between the wickets

"My first instinct wa to rush straight to th scene with my first ai kit," said Mr. Adams, wh is a senior Red Cro

Len Hutton only two overs to be convinced that the pitch at Chesterfield in 1946 was the wrong length. After careful measurements were taken, it was found that play in the Derbyshire v. Yorkshire match had begun on a pitch 24 yards long. The groundstaff rapidly drew in new lines to the correct length, and the match was restarted.

For **human interruptions of the violent kind** we have to travel East again, stopping first at Karachi where City Gymkhana and Nazimabad Sports were in play. At the crease were the former Test cricketer Saladhuddin and Prince Aslam, who was renowned for his fiery temper. An appeal for l.b.w. against the Prince was upheld by the umpire, despite strong protests from the volatile batsman. The umpire remained firm, and the Prince had to walk. Minutes later, after he had smouldered for a while in the pavilion, the Prince was back on the pitch, now carrying a loaded revolver which he fired once in the air above the umpire's head. The effect was dramatic. Prince Aslam's reputation being well known, the batsmen, fielders and umpires fled the field, jumped over a fence and vanished. The match was abandoned.

During another match involving Nazimabad Sports, a one-day game against Clifton Gymkhana, four motorcyclists suddenly roared on to the pitch from different directions. Leaping off, the riders seized the captain of Clifton Gymkhana, the Test cricketer Aftab Baloch, and forcibly shaved his hair. Knowing that the assailants carried knives, none of the other players – who included another Test player, Mohsin Khan – nor the umpires dared to interfere. Later it transpired that Aftab had been set on because he had dropped a player who was so offended that he called in the heavy mob to exact revenge.

Only one man is on record as having won the George Cross on the cricket field. He is Colonel Douglas Brett, who in 1934 was playing in a match at Chittagong when five Hindu terrorists – four of them carrying bombs and the other firing a pistol – charged on to the field and began

g on Curdridge cricket pitch, pictured by Royal Marine Commando Michael Hillier.

ell as being Curdridge uncil and the village's Committee nsibility for pitch. as wonderful. was falling laughter and hurt." the delighted Curdridge's ure with the

Medstead XI was Michael Hillier, of the Commando Logistics Regiment of the Royal Marines, currently on leave with his wife and baby at his home in Curdridge.

Based at Plymouth, he flew home from the Falk-

land Islands to Brize Norton on July 14.

"I have never seen anything like it in my life. I just had to grab my camera and take a few shots," said the 22-year-old whose twin brother Nicholas was playing for Curdridge.

Balloon stopped play at Curdridge, near Southampton, when a hot-air balloon advertising a new burger restaurant ran out of fuel sooner than expected and was brought down to land neatly between the stumps during a match in 1982 between Curdridge and Medstead.

attacking both players and spectators. Colonel Brett, less daunted than others present, waded in with a one-man counter-attack. For his courage he was awarded the Empire Gallantry Medal, the holders of which were automatically awarded the George Cross when this medal was instituted in 1940.

The **only kangaroo to possess a complete M.C.C. outfit** has yet to create a disruption in play, but if it ever does find its way to a cricket ground, disruption there will surely be. The kangaroo's interest in the M.C.C. began in January 1981 when a *bona fide* member went on a trip in the Australian bush in a hired car fitted with the regular steel bars above the front bumper, to prevent the bonnet from being smashed on impact with a kangaroo. After touring for a few

Protest in the Parks: a crowd of anti-apartheid demonstrators held up play in the 1969 match between Oxford University and Wilfred Isaac's all-white South African touring team. The stumps were ripped up at one end and forty minutes' playing time was lost before, with light police intervention, the cricketers could resume.

days without incident, they suddenly collided with a kangaroo which bounded in front of the car while it was travelling at 60 m.p.h. Apparently the kangaroo died instantly. To commemorate the incident, the driver and his friend hauled the 'roo to its feet and decked it out with M.C.C. tie, cap and blazer prior to taking a photograph of the animal. While the member was checking his camera the kangaroo suddenly revived and made off into the bush where, presumably, it still sports the flamboyant colours of the Marylebone Cricket Club.

Cricket in Fiji is not spared from local customs. In his book *Cricket in the Fiji Islands*, published in 1949, Philip Snow reported the **bizarre mourning ritual** witnessed by Sir Basil Thomson, then an administrative officer in the islands and later head of the C.I.D. at Scotland Yard.

'In Lau I had a good example of the hold which formalism and ceremony have upon the people. The island of Lakeba had sent a cricket team to play Lomaloma. The match was about even, and there was a large body of spectators from both islands to watch the second innings. Suddenly a messenger arrived from the beach and approached the Lakeba captain who was bowling. I was near enough to overhear the conversation. The messenger had just landed from a fast sailing cutter to bring the news of the sudden death of the chief's brother, who was the uncle of the Lakeba captain and of many of the native ladies assembled at the scoring-table. Play stopped: the captain walked over to the group and gravely announced the news. "Will you weep now or wait till the innings is over?" he asked. The women consulted and said: "Go on with the match. We will do our weeping afterwards." So back we went to play as if nothing had happened. When the last wicket had fallen, and I had almost forgotten the incident, a piercing wail broke from the scoring-table. It was taken up by all the Lakeba women. They were howling with open mouths: tears were rolling down their cheeks: they tore their hair and scratched their faces and breasts, and when the orgy of ceremonial grief seemed to be dying down from exhaustion, a fresh shriek would set it all going again. I looked at the faces of their mankind: they were quite unconcerned and impassive, and so were those of the Lomaloma women. I met the mourners later in the afternoon; they were laughing and talking as usual, and there was nothing about them but unhealed scratches to remind me of their tragic concession to ancient custom.'

Finally, two examples of breaks in play being carried to a fine point of absurdity. First, the **longest lunch interval.** This was registered in the month of October in a match between the Gentlemen of Coolatin and Halverstown. After a delayed start the first ball was bowled at 12.45 and Halverstown were all out by 1.30 for 17. Lunch was taken in the local hotel and lasted $4\frac{1}{2}$ hours. By this time dusk was falling, neither side was at its most accurate and eight Coolatin wickets fell before the winning hit was made in pitch darkness.

The **longest-ever cricket match** lasted 20 years. The teams met at Avondale Park, Galveston every year on 4 June and played until one wicket fell. They then walked off and resumed the match the following year.

·FAMILY· CONNECTIONS

Cricket can never have run in the family quite so fluently as it did with the Robinsons of Backwell House, Gloucestershire. They fielded a team every season for 80 years between 1878 and 1957, with interruptions permitted only for the two world wars. Altogether the team played 144 matches, and every member of the side was a Robinson.

The Edrich family of Norfolk, five of whom played first-class cricket and two of whom, the cousins Bill and John, appeared many times for England, have often also fielded a family team.

In Denmark the magic name is Morild. Since the Danes played their first international in 1954, no side has taken the field without a member of the Morild family in it. Best aggregate was in 1959 for the match against Holland, when four Morilds played. As for continuity between the generations, when Carsten Morild made his début in 1955 his father Svend was also in the side. Twenty-three years later, when Claus Morild appeared for his country for the first time, his father Carsten was still in the team.

The Amarnaths of India have possibly the **most distinguished record at Test level,** being the only family in which a father and son have scored a century on their débuts. In the 1933–34 season Lala Amarnath hit 118 against England in the first-ever Test played in India. No such success awaited the now famous Mohinder on his début in 1969–70, but his brother Surinder fared better in 1975–76, scoring 124 in his first Test on the Indians' tour of New Zealand.

The feats for Australia of the Chappell brothers Ian, Greg and Trevor are better known than the fact that their grandfather, Victor Richardson, also played for his country and captained the side on five occasions. Although Ian and Greg played for different state sides, this did not prevent them from registering the oddest batting 'double' in Sheffield Shield cricket. In the 1973–74 season, they hit an identical total of runs in their two matches against Victoria:

Greg	180 and 101 at Brisbane
	115 and 53* at Melbourne
Ian	83 and 95 at Melbourne
	141* and 130 at Adelaide

These performances gave them 449 runs each for the same average: 149.66.

In 1977, when J. G. Tolchard stepped in to keep wicket for Leicestershire against Derbyshire at Burton-on-Trent in place of his injured brother R. W., the regular 'keeper, he was helping to set a **bizarre stumper's record** – the first incidence of two brothers keeping wicket for the same county throughout a County Championship game.

The brothers Steele set a first in 1971 when, playing for opposing sides, each scored a century. J. F. Steele hit 123 for Leicestershire while his brother D. S. Steele scored 107* for Northamptonshire. In 1973 they repeated the performance when, at Northampton, J. F. scored 118 and his brother 116.

Only once have brothers taken a hat-trick in the same innings. David and Derek Preston opened the bowling in 1977 for Long Lee against Morton in the West Bradford League, collected a hat-trick apiece and Morton were returned to the pavilion for 28.

A bizarre line in the scorecard at Lord's for the 1933 match between Middlesex and Somerset read:

H. W. Lee   c. F. S. Lee   b. J. W. Lee   82

All three were, of course, brothers.

The Bedsers, Alec and Eric, are **first-class cricket's most famous twins.** In addition to the Surrey pair, there have been three other 'sets' of twins: J. S. and W. H. Denton (Northants), A. D. E. and A. E. S. Rippon (Somerset) and F. G. and W. H. Stephens (Warwicks).

Sussex have a rich tradition of **fathers, sons and brothers** playing for the county, and one instance of three Lillywhites – grandfather, father and son – all appearing in the same match. The Langridges, James and John, remain the only brothers to score 2,000 runs in the same first-class season (1937), and in 1930 H. W. and J. H. Parks each scored a century in the same innings, against Lancashire at Eastbourne, and that year each reached 1,000 runs in the same match, against Kent at Hastings. J. H. Parks's son Jim played for England as a batsman and wicketkeeper, and *his* son Bobby is now the Hampshire wicketkeeper.

Father and son have also scored a century in the same innings. They were the Gunns of Nottinghamshire, who in 1931 registered this unique feat against Warwickshire at Birmingham. G. Gunn scored 183 and his son G. V. hit 100 not out.

Worcestershire, of course, had their Fosters, seven in all representing the county. Five of the brothers played regularly in 1908. In Worcestershire's first County Championship match, in 1899, three Fosters were present – H. K., R. E. and W. L. The last of the Foster brothers to play in a county match was M. K., in 1934.

In the Oval Test of 1983 five of the New Zealand XI, including the Crowe brothers Jeff and Martin, had brothers who were Test cricketers. Richard Hadlee – whose father Walter as well as his brother Dale played in Tests – John Bracewell and Geoff Howarth were the others.

To end, a zoomorphic record from Yorkshire, where in 1981 two ducks bowled to two swans. During a York Senior League match brothers Colin and Ken Swann of Tadcaster faced up to New Earswick's captain John Duck and his son Stephen.

The Bedser
twins, Alec (left)
and Eric.

Joan and
Barbara Blaker,
the cricketing
twins from
Eltham, with
Australia's
captain
Mrs Peden
in 1937.

What the Graces were to Gloucestershire and England, the Newhalls were to Philadelphia and the United States. In 1901 they fielded a complete family side against Baltimore.

Two Langridges, John (left) and James.

MOST RUNS OFF ONE BALL

This intriguing sub-category of 'Bizarre Batting Records' deserves a chapter to itself simply because of the wonderful variety of mishaps witnessed in its name. The **most outrageous claim** is for the first hit in a match played at Bonbury, Western Australia, either in December 1893 or January 1894, between a team from Victoria and a local side.

 The Victorians batted first and the opening delivery was slammed into a three-pronged branch of a tall jarrah tree. As the visiting batsmen scampered between the stumps the home side appealed for 'lost ball', but were overruled by the umpire who said it was not lost because it was still in view. The West Australians sent for an axe to cut down the tree but in the urgency of the moment no axe could be found. Someone eventually brought a rifle and the best shot in the home team was deputed to knock down the ball. After several misses, down came the ball – but no-one thought to catch it. The Victorians claimed, and got, 286 runs for the hit, and declared. This target was too much for the home side.

 A similar incident occurred in South London in 1894. Camberwell Albion scored 129 all out, leaving Peckham Pushers only 55 minutes to get the runs. Their opening batsman J. H. Brown hit the first ball of the innings into a tree growing inside the boundary. Again the ball was visible, though this time it had lodged in a rook's nest. Brown and his partner, A. Archer, ran 93 while the ball was retrieved. Encouraged by this useful start, the Pushers won by four wickets.

 In a match played in the Solomon Islands the ball was hit into the sea – which was evidently regarded as in play, so the batsmen carried on running. After some hot debate about who should fetch it, possibly because **killer fish patrolled those waters,** it was decided that the nearest fielder to the point of entry would be ideal, and square-leg was thrown in. By the time the ball was returned to the stumps the batsmen had run 56.

A rival English claim goes 11 better than the Solomon Islanders' feat. Whether word of the earlier Australian performance had filtered through to Rottingdean in Sussex, and been ignored, is not known, but the Sussex club say that the hit for 67 made on their Beacon Hill ground is a world record. The club played on that ground all through the 19th century and up to 1914, and at some unspecified date a batsman struck a lofted drive down the hill and into the village where it was retrieved by a relay of fielders. Unfortunately, the last man overthrew and the ball ran off down the other side of the hill while the **batsmen on the summit** tore triumphantly back and forth.

On a more modest scale, but no less memorable to the batsman concerned, D. H. R. Martin completed the only century he ever scored with a hit for 14. He was playing for Oriel Orphans v. Radley 2nd XI at Radley in about 1928. Several games were in progress side by side on the same field when Martin, then on 87, hit the ball into a neighbouring game. Whether by design or accident, the fielder in that game picked up the ball and flung it as hard as he could in the opposite direction, and Martin dashed on to 101.

ANIMAL HAVOC

Dogs merely trespassing on the pitch, like schoolboys darting about inside the boundary ropes, are not the currency of this chapter. Qualifying animals must by their intervention change the course of the game. A good example is the **snake at the wicket** in Johannesburg which so terrified batsmen Pieter Marrish that he would not return to the crease and was run out.

Delicate feelings of a less mortal nature cost Worcester Nomads several runs in a match against the villagers of Moor, near Evesham. One of the home side's batsmen cleverly stroked the ball **into a cowpat,** and the nearest fielder was highly reluctant to retrieve it. While the Moor batsmen crossed and recrossed many times, no Nomads came to the help of their teammate, but were content to roast him verbally from a distance. At last the fielder was persuaded to sacrifice his handkerchief, which he dropped over the ball and then, quickly lifting the malodorous parcel, flung it in the general direction of the wicketkeeper.

Animals can intimidate fielders by reputation alone. During World War I two teams of soldiers were playing a match when a bunch of **untethered mules** strayed inside the boundary. The batsman landed a shot in the middle of

them, and he and his partner gathered a goodly pile of runs while the fielders dithered on the fringe of the mule pack, overawed by these animals' reputation for hefty kicking when annoyed.

At Undercliffe, around that same period, a donkey used to pull the roller. Until, that is, a team from Lidget Green visited Undercliffe for a Priestley Cup-tie. They were quick to notice that the wicket at one end was much wetter than at the other, and they immediately protested. When questioned by the League executive, the groundsman admitted that in the course of its duties before the game, and while still harnessed to the roller, the **donkey had been taken short.** The League executive ordered the game to be replayed and Undercliffe were banned from playing any Cup matches at home for the rest of that season. What may have encouraged a penalty of such severity was the fact that the wetted end was the one to which Cecil Parkin always bowled – though how this tactical point might have been conveyed to the donkey no-one could explain.

The **ball-snatching variety of dog,** as opposed to the mere trespasser, has caused a good deal of havoc on the cricket field, no small part of which is the arguing provoked over how many runs should be awarded while the ball was in its mouth. In a match played in 1925 at Palmerston North, New Zealand, E. R. Mayne was batting for the touring Victorian State side against Manawatu and struck the ball past mid-on who gave chase. So too did a fox-terrier which rushed on from the boundary, captured the ball and made off with it. While the Manawatu players sprinted after the weaving fox-terrier, Mayne and his partner took 11 runs and then the dog carried the ball over the boundary. Mayne's claim to 11 runs was hotly contested by the Manawatu side who said he should have four for the 'boundary' shot, and no more. The umpires were in high confusion since they could find no rule in the book to cover what had happened. Mayne sportingly offered to back down and accepted four.

This was the verdict in similar incidents recorded at Dulverton, Somerset during a village match (when the dog was a small white terrier and made its dash from behind deep square leg) and at Hove when Sussex played the West Indians in 1963 and the batsman was A. L. Valentine. No description has survived of the Hove dog but it is interesting to note that it too attacked from square leg. More research is needed before it can be firmly asserted that dogs respond more positively to balls coming off the bat at a right-angle from the bowler's line of delivery; but the possibility is there, and may be linked to mounting evidence that more dogs of the ball-snatching variety wait on the square-leg boundary than in any other part of the field.

The 'lost ball' rule has entered several dog-snatches-ball incidents. In 1893 W. H. Martin ran 12 for Cobham against Thames Ditton but the umpire only allowed him four. This would be an incorrect decision today, since under Law 21 the batsman is entitled to at least six runs if the ball is lost, i.e. it 'cannot be found or recovered'. Moreover, if the fielding side fails to claim 'lost ball', the batsman may score as many runs as have been run.

In a match on the Nottingham Forest ground in 1892, the invading dog must have made a lightning approach – unless it had been lurking on the field already – since it intercepted a defensive prod back to the bowler, then eluded the field while the batsmen took 10 runs. The fielders claimed 'lost ball' but the batsmen argued that it was not lost since it was visible. Their plea convinced the umpires and they kept their 10.

Birds have a less joyful relationship with cricket and cricket balls, which almost invariably strike them while in flight, with fatal effect. It is unusual for the deadly blow to affect the course of the game, but it has been known. H. Tubb, of Rugby and Oxford, kept and **stuffed a swift** that was struck and killed by a young farmer-batsman in a match at Bicester. On this occasion the impact with the bird deflected the ball into the hands of a fielder and the farmer was given out caught. B. W. Bentinck, playing for Alton in 1923, was unlucky enough to be bowled by a ball which hit a passing swallow and veered onto the stumps.

The Australian Test batsman John Inverarity was more fortunate. He too, in an inter-state match in 1969, was bowled by a ball which ricocheted off a bird onto the wicket, but the umpire had called a no-ball.

Derek Morgan, the Derbyshire all-rounder, had cause to thank a sharp-eyed umpire in the match at Hastings in 1959 between England and a

Commonwealth XI. His leg stump was knocked back by a ball from Les Jackson but he was allowed to remain at the wicket because the umpire noticed, just as the ball was being bowled, that he had drawn back to avoid a wasp that flew across his face.

Two swallows were caught by fielders in a match at Woodstock, near Cape Town, between the home side and the Royal Artillery. The fielders were Sergeant McGwire and Corporal Messenger, both of whom claimed they had snatched at the dark fast-moving object because they **thought it was the ball.** Neither appeal was allowed to stand.

Bob Willis inspects a stunned seagull, laid out by a drive from Australian Keith Stackpole; the bird was later taken off for treatment.

BIZARRE LINES FROM THE SCOREBOOK

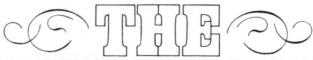

Proof positive of the 'unique record' of the two teams who each represented Bollington and Winnington Park on 6 July 1929.

Bollington Cricket Club.
UNIQUE RECORD.
BOLLINGTON FIRST V. WINNINGTON PARK FIRST.
AT WINNINGTON PARK, JULY 6TH, 1929.

Bollington Innings.

J H Jackson b Stephenson	5
H Compston c Ellis b Stephenson	4
Cook c Hyland b Stephenson	3
W Goodwin c Guthrie b Williams	52
T Cooper b Hyland	0
Jos. Jackson run out	9
J Bowden b Hyland	7
H Heywood b Hyland	3
T N Turner c Guthrie b Williams	0
H Clay c Ellis b Hyland	0
C Bray not out	4
Extras	
Total	**89**

Winnington Innings.

A Guthrie c Jackson b Cook	6
H Guthrie c Compston b Cook	15
T B Woodcock b Bowden	0
W H Lamb b Bowden	4
J Stephenson b Cook	0
W Williams lbw b Bowden	23
J C Ellis b Turner	16
J Wynne c Cook b Turner	3
F Hodkinson c Clay b Cook	0
K Ellis c Goodwin b Cook	3
F Hyland not out	
Extras	
Total	**89**

Bowling.

	O.	M.	R.	W.
Hylands	19	6	28	4
Stephenson	14	6	43	3
Williams	4	0	14	2

	O.	M.	R.	W.
Cook	24.2	11	34	5
Heywood	12	2	21	0
Turner	13	5	20	2
Bowden	4	1	11	3

— SECOND TEAMS AT BOLLINGTON.

Bollington.

C Goodwin c Stelfox b Norcross	1
B Harwood st Dale b Norcross	
A Wainwright c Gallimore b Norcross	0
E Stewart lbw b Manning	33
W Jones b Stelfox	14
J Vare c Dale b Stelfox	5
A Bowden c Gallimore b Stelfox	6
J Nolan lbw b Stelfox	0
B Cooper not out	
H Furness st Dale b Norcross	
T L Jackson c & b Bebbington	7
Extras	
Total	**83**

Winnington.

S Bebbington c Jones b Nolan	12
F Gallimore c Stewart b Furness	15
E Stelfox c Bowden b Furness	6
A Dale c Jones b Cooper	4
W R D Manning b Furness	0
C Hughes c Jackson b Cooper	28
J Clarke c Cooper b Stewart	6
B Gallimore c Nolan b Cooper	2
A R Cashmore c Goodwin b Stewart	0
L Wilkinson not out	5
F Norcross c Furness b Cooper	3
Extras	
Total	**83**

Bowling.

	O.	M.	R.	W.
Bebbington	10	6	17	1
Norcross	12	4	31	4
Stelfox	8	3	16	4
Manning	5	0	12	1

	O.	M.	R.	W.
J Vare	2	0	16	0
B Cooper	6.2	3	25	3
H Furness	7	1	20	3
J Nolan	5	2	10	1
T L Jackson	2	1	10	0
E Stewart	8	3	8	2

Chadwick, Printer, Bollington

We have known for some time that coincidence has a long arm, and cricket is by nature the kind of game which hurls out statistics from the moment the first ball is bowled. Even so, it continues to amaze us to what extent that long arm has invaded the scorebooks, inscribing lines far too preposterous for the most romantic sort of fiction.

At times we are tempted to suspect a plot; collusion among the players. For instance, Bollington 1st XI travelled to Winnington Park on 6 July 1929 to play Winnington Park 1st XI. Each side scored 89 and the match was tied. On the same day, Winnington Park 2nd XI went to Bollington to play the home club's 2nd XI. Each side scored 83, so that match also was tied.

Our Resident Sceptic on the Square-leg Boundary: 'Something fishy there, eh?'

His Companion, a Statistician: 'Not at all. Pure coincidence.'·

Sceptic: 'Trying to get themselves into the record books, more like.'

Statistician: 'Impossible. Well, not impossible, but forty-four payers and four umpires at two separate grounds could hardly have contrived such an outcome deliberately.'

Sceptic: 'Too much of a coincidence, do you mean?'

Statistician: 'No, there's no such thing. The point is, surely, that cricket produces enough odd statistics, it would be a waste of time to go around faking them.'

Sceptic: 'The whole crew of them should be locked up.'

Statistician: 'If you said that each time a coincidence happened, the players would soon all be inside and you wouldn't have any cricket to watch.'

Sceptic (grumpily): 'Still seems fishy to me.' (Pause) 'What kind of sandwiches did you bring today?'

The improbability of it all seems to be what intrigues people most, sparking debates not just in the lunch interval but into the evening and through the winter as well. To a degree, it has become competitive, with statisticians rootling among scorebooks ancient and modern in quest of further oddities. Thanks to their eternal curiosity we can report no less than four instances of ties in which the opposing teams made the same score in each innings. In chronological order, they were:

1818. Woking v. Shere. Both sides scored 71 twice.

1885. Tenby v. Royal Fusiliers. Both sides scored 51 twice.

1929. Totteridge v. Fortress. Both sides scored 94 twice.

1982. Heathcote Schoolboys v. Cronulla RSL Club. Both sides scored 55 twice.

No level of the game is unaffected. Bizarre scores and averages befall the great as well as the humble. In the Third Test at Auckland between New Zealand and Pakistan in 1973, both teams scored 402 in their 1st innings; the top-scorers on each side, B. F. Hastings and Majid Khan, both got 110. Meanwhile, that same week in Kingston, Jamaica, Australia and West Indies both scored 428 in their 1st innings.

Bev Congdon, captain of that 1973 New Zealand side, emerged from the match against Pakistan with a batting average of 30 (24 and 6 not out). In 1973–74 he toured Australia and had identical batting and bowling averages in the

Test series: 30.00. He thus shared the experience of A. E. Relf, who in the M.C.C. tour of South Africa in 1905–06 scored 404 in 16 completed innings, took 16 wickets for 404 runs and finished with a double average of 25.25.

Two great batsmen who dogged each other's footsteps in first-class matches in 1981 were Viv Richards and Clive Lloyd. Both finished as follows: Innings 31 Not out 2 Runs 1324 Average 45.65.

MOST INFORMATIVE SCOREBOARD

'It must be the ages of the bowlers, not their numbers in the batting order.'

'I didn't know Molesworth was 28.'

No such conversation took place in the 1974 match between Aravon Prep School, Bray, Co. Wicklow and Old Aravonians. The bottom line of this initially mystifying scoreboard is in fact most informative and carries details, on the left, of the winning score of the British Lions in the 2nd Test v. South Africa; the figures on the right represent the current score in the 2nd cricket Test between England and India.

More double-takes. In a county match between Middlesex and Warwickshire in 1970 both sides included a player called Smith whose first two initials were M. J. Both wore glasses and both scored 53.

In the Bradford League in 1982, David Jay of Manningham Mills returned figures of 6–1–41–0 on successive days, against Bingley and Hanging Heaton. On both days he conceded sixes off the second, third and fourth balls of his last over.

The Second Test in 1977 between England and Australia began at Old Trafford on 7-7-77, the 77th day of the Australians' tour. In the 77th over, Doug Walters took his score to 77; his partner was Rodney Marsh, No 7 in the Australian order.

On 19 January 1982 the scoreboard at 3.33 p.m. at the Sydney Cricket Ground made interesting reading (West Indies batting against Australia):

Viv Richards	33
Faoud Bacchus	3
Extras	3
Wickets	3
Last Man (L. Gomes)	3
Greg Chappell	0–3

Later that year, on 10 December 1982, the scoreboard immediately following John Dyson's dismissal in the Adelaide Test against England contained the following figures:

K. Wessels c. Taylor b. Botham	44
J. Dyson c. Taylor b. Botham	44
G. Chappell not out	44
R. Willis	0–44

We suspect there may be more where that came from!

Cricketers need to be at least 50 before they can be considered ancients of the game. After that there is no stopping some, who may go on for a further half century, being pavilioned in splendour, girded with praise, and quietly cursed by youths of 38 and 40 who cannot get a place in the team because of them.

In Warwickshire the name of William Quaife stands at the head of many county records. He began his first-class career in 1894, the same year as his brother Walter, but while Walter finished in 1901 William went on until 1928. In his last county championship match, against Derbyshire, he was 56 years and 4 months old; he batted once and scored 115, which established him as the **oldest century-maker in first-class county cricket.** Not surprisingly, he also made many more appearances for the county (665) than any other player (F. R. Santall, the next-longest server, made 496); scored more centuries (71) and hit 1,000 runs in a season more often (20 times); his aggregate of runs is also the county's highest by some way, at 33,862.

The evergreen William Lillywhite, a pioneer of round-arm bowling.

Probably the **oldest opening bowler in first-class cricket** was William Lillywhite, who was 61 when in July 1853 he opened for Sussex v. England with a tidy spell of 11 overs, from which 23 runs were scored.

Outside the county game a contemporary of William Quaife, F. W. Stancomb, may be the **longest-serving captain.** Not content with merely playing for Trowbridge C.C., he then became their captain in 1876 and stayed in that office for 50 years.

Now we are in pensioner country. Candidate for the **most ancient newcomer** is Laurie Pullen, who joined Bledlow C.C. in 1982 at the age of 67 and played regular 1st XI cricket for them in the Chiltern League.

W. Jones remained a demon bowler until he was at least 66. In 1938, playing for Eastwood Belfairs and West Leigh, he took 292 wickets for 7.8 runs apiece. Althogether he took 100 or more wickets in a season 37 times.

Oldest bowler to achieve a hat-trick is very likely Rev. J. F. Denning of Hungerford, who in 1927 took four wickets in four balls at the age of 73. The previous season his total bag was 214 wickets. Rev. Denning's feats are especially interesting in that he did not take to cricket until he was 34.

Most of the *real* ancients belong to previous ages. In fact, the match featuring the **oldest collection of cricketers** may have been played as long ago as Restoration Day 1727, when 12 men over 70 took part in a game at Cranbrook. The oldest was 84 and two were 82. The Cranbrook match is challenged for the longevity of its players by a 12-a-side game at Saltaire Park, near Bradford, in 1914 between Chellow Dene and Shipley. The average age of the players was 75, the oldest being 87.

A player whose career spanned almost the entire Victorian age was Charles Absolon, the Grand Old Man of London club cricket who may also be the **most impressive septuagenarian all-rounder** in the history of the game. He played until he was 80, in which season (1897) he took 100 wickets. When he was 75 he took 200 wickets, and 209 when he was 76. An early highlight was a match at Wallingford on 28 June 1838, Queen Victoria's Coronation Day, when he played for Butchers v. Bakers. Such was his enthusiasm for cricket, he sometimes played in two matches in one day. Underarm lob bowling was his strength, but he also made his share of runs. In his last 30 playing years he took 8,500 wickets and scored 26,000 runs. He played with W. G. and E. M. Grace when they were schoolboys, and against four generations of the cricketing Bentley family. A final statistic from Charles Absolon's remarkable record: he performed the hat-trick 59 times between 1871 and 1893.

Octogenarian cricketers are thinner on the ground nowadays, though they can be found in unexpected places. Two Europeans who played with distinction until about 1970 were the Dutchman Dr A. F. H. Lobry de Bruyn and Thomas Morild, a Dane. The Dutchman was still taking wickets after his 80th birthday, even though his deliveries were remarkably slow through the air. Thomas Morild, doyen of his country's most famous cricketing family, played his last match on his 81st birthday. Afterwards there was a party, and it is said that he was one of the last to leave that as well. In his native town of Hjørring the street leading to the cricket ground is named after him.

Moving **into the nineties** we find G. White, aged 92, going out to receive the first ball in a match to celebrate the opening of the new ground at Purbrook, Portsmouth, in 1922. He had first played for Purbrook C.C. seventy years before.

More triumphant still was the feat of John Durant, said to be 103 when in 1913 he bowled the opening ball in a charity match between Weybridge XX and G. W. Ayres XVI. The ball lured the great Surrey player Tom Hayward out of his ground and he was stumped.

In the matter of old age, umpires too can keep their end up. John Stewart, a former Chairman of the Association of Cricket Umpires, gave 50 years' continuous service and stood in 2,498 games – 92 in his last season. Another to complete 50 years of umpiring was Arthur Hughesman, of Birchington C.C., who reached his half-century in 1975 at the age of 82.

Arthur Barrett of Harrogate umpired for 65 years in the Yorkshire Council despite having an artificial leg, after being wounded in World War I in the Battle of Vimy Ridge. In 1982, at the age of 86, he was still officiating in the Harrogate area, this being his 68th season as an umpire.

The final award, for the **oldest umpire,** goes to Joe Philliston, of North London, who in the 1960s officiated on his 100th birthday.

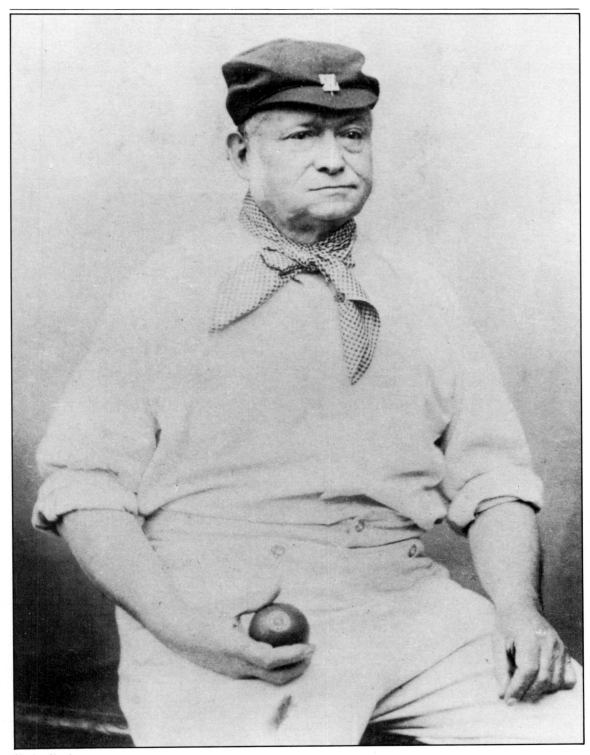

Charles Absolon

MOST DRAMATIC TURNAROUNDS

When **lunatic fluctuations** are in the air, four innings are better than two, and so it is to the County Championship that we first look. Hampshire v. Warwickshire at Edgbaston in 1922 is a deservedly famous example of the genre, for in that match the ultimate victors also managed to register the county's lowest-ever score.

After Warwickshire had scored an unremarkable 223, they skittled Hampshire for 15 in 8.5 overs. The dependable Mead managed 6 not out but none of his teammates could withstand the bowling of Howell (6 for 7) and Calthorpe (4 for 4). Following on, Hampshire were still behind with six second innings wickets down, but first Brown (172) and Livsey (110 not out) put on 177 for the ninth wicket and then Livsey and Boyes scored 70 for the last wicket and Hampshire finished with a total of 521. Kennedy and Newman dismissed Warwickshire for 158 and Hampshire won by 155 runs.

At Southport in 1982, Warwickshire were again embarrassed. In their first innings they scored 523 for 4 dec., which included a record 4th wicket stand of 470 by Alvin Kallicharran (230) and Geoff Humpage (254). They then went on to lose the match to Lancashire by 10 wickets, Graham Fowler scoring a century in each innings – another bizarre record since he batted throughout with a runner.

Only two Test matches have ever been won by a side after following on. England achieved this v. Australia at Sydney in 1894–95 and at Headingley in 1981 – 'Botham's match'.

In the 1927 Championship, scoring was by a percentage method and Nottinghamshire had only to avoid defeat at Swansea to become champions. Confidence in the Trent Bridge camp was high: Glamorgan had not won a single match that season, and the county committee booked a band to welcome the side home after the trip to Swansea.

On the first day Notts batted stolidly through to the close for 233 all out. Glamorgan then hit a rapid 375 (W. E. Bates 163) and by the end of the second day had the Notts openers Gunn and Whysall out for 14. In the night it rained heavily, producing an insoluble 'sticky' on which the putative champions-elect collapsed for 61, Mercer taking 6 for 31 and Ryan 4 for 14. The defeat let in Lancashire at the head of the county table.

Whether a game was enjoyably 'fantastic' or an unfortunate 'freak' tends to be a matter of viewpoint. To the reporter of the *Watford Observer* the turnaround between Bushey and Watford Grammar School in 1959 was worth a pile of superlatives. Under the heading 'BOWLED OUT FOR THIRTY – THEN FORCE WIN IN FANTASTIC GAME' was the following report:

'Strangest game of the cricketing weekend? The one at the Moat Field, Bushey, on Saturday must qualify for that description for without one player reaching double figures the home side were bowled out for 30 by Watford Grammar School's K. Morley (8 for 15) and W. Hedger (2 for 14).

'The School were undoubtedly pleased with themselves, and happier still when their opening pair, J. Swain (15) and R. Gilchrist (11), put on 24 for the first wicket.

'But Bushey had the last laugh. Thanks to the excellent bowling of Robin Leach, who took seven for 3 in five overs, including five wickets in seven balls and a hat-trick, and finished the game with an analysis of 7 for 10, the rest of

NEXT!

the School batsmen were shot out for the addition of only five runs. This gave Bushey a win by one run in what can only be described as a fantastic finish.'

After giving the match due thought, the editors of the School Magazine summed it up in their review of the season with the comment: 'This game is best written off as a freak.'

One of the **briefest-ever local derbies** must have been that between the Devonshire town of South Molton and the nearby village of North Molton in 1963. North Molton batted first and were all out for 6 in 10.1 overs; South Molton's opening bowler Brian Tapp took all 10 wickets for 1 run. The town side thought the rest would be the merest pushover . . . until 10.1 overs later when their last wicket fell with their total also on 6.

JUMPING BAILS

If Man at the Crease is a figure much prone to accident, then so is the woodwork before which he stands. In theory this should not be so. Stumps and bails are designed with a beautiful symmetry: provided they are the correct height and width, the stumps being of equal size, broad enough to prevent the ball from passing through, and driven firmly into the ground so that the bails fit perfectly in the grooves awaiting them; provided all this is done according to the book, what could go wrong? Furthermore, in a high wind the laws of the game allow for the captains to agree, with the approval of the umpires, to dispense with the use of bails. It all seems to be buttoned up pretty tightly.

The laws of disaster and the bizarre decree otherwise. Bails do not always spring off in the manner expected of them. Stumps are not always the regulation distance apart. The game, regrettably, is littered with examples of the latter. Even in 1853, when British engineers had just scaled new peaks of achievement at the Great Exhibition in Hyde Park, the stumps at Ipswich were not what they should have been. W. Caffyn, playing for the All England XI v. XXII of Ipswich, threw in the ball from long-off and saw it pass through the stumps at the bowler's end, bound down the pitch and go between the stumps at the other end.

In Australia the middle stump was bowled out of the ground during a match between New South Wales and Victoria but the bails remained rigidly in position. The sun had melted the varnish on them and they were glued to the remaining stumps. Since neither the captains nor the umpires had any prior knowledge of this, there had been no question of dispensing with the bails, and to the chagrin of the bowler the verdict had to be: not out.

The *Sporting Magazine* reported in 1822 that in a match between Navestock and Pattiswick in Essex the ball struck a stump and the bail leapt from its groove – only to fall back there and come to rest again as though nothing had happened. The umpire's verdict is not recorded, but in similar circumstances in 1931 the batsman was given out bowled. The occasion was a county match between Northamptonshire and Glamorgan, and the Northants batsman A. H. Bakewell was the unhappy victim. The impact of the ball knocked the bail out of its groove but it then swivelled and stopped without falling. The umpire's decision was correct under an M.C.C. ruling of 1929.

By an extraordinary coincidence, a match between Manchester and Old Trafford in 1883 yielded two instances of erratic bail behaviour. First a bail jumped from its perch then lodged between the splayed off stump and the middle stump, and later in the match a bail was dislodged from its groove but did not fall.

Truly acrobatic bails have been sighted on more than one occasion. In 1882 Rev. T. G. Dale bowled a lob to W. Hearn which hit the top of the off stump and removed the off bail. The leg bail came to rest lying on top of the leg stump, and reversed.

More recently, in a match between Selsey and Radio Solent, Selsey's opening bowler contrived to knock both the leg and off stumps out of the ground. The middle stump was left standing with a bail spinning round on top of it. The bail slowed down gradually and stopped, still balanced on the stump, pointing jointly at the bowler and the wicketkeeper.

In a bizarre sequence in another match, the batsman advanced down the pitch and drove the ball straight to the bowler who stopped it smartly and returned it even more smartly while the batsman was still out of his ground. The bowler's aim was not true, but a close fielder still managed to touch the ball on to the wicket, where it lodged between the middle and leg stumps without removing a bail. By then, the batsman had scuttled home, so no appeal followed; but the fielders may well have felt that their enterprise had been poorly rewarded.

At Lord's in 1893 the Middlesex player C. P. Foley picked up a bail from the ground and was dismayed to be **given out 'handled bail'.** He was trailing back to the pavilion before the Sussex captain W. L. Murdoch overruled the umpire's decision and asked Foley to resume at the wicket.

In his farewell match a batsman may perhaps be forgiven for being over-protective towards his wicket. Making his last appearance for Chorleywood in 1972, John Swain had scored 43 when he used a hand to stop the ball from going on to his stumps. In response to appeals from the fielding side, the umpire at the bowler's end said it was not out, and the square-leg umpire said it was. Swain, incorrectly it seems, stayed and went on to make 79.

All sorts of batting equipment – gloves, bats, caps, helmets, even spectacles – have fallen on the stumps and been the instrument of downfall for many a hapless batsman. It must be even worse to be **undone by a piece of string.**

This was the fate of Captain Johnson of the 50th Regiment, playing in 1886 at Woolwich for Mr Fowler's XI v. Royal Artillery. As he cut a ball for two runs, the string binding at the bottom of his bat came loose and about three feet of it unravelled on the ground while he was running. Unaware of the loose string – which no-one else sought to draw to his attention – he played a similar cut stroke at the next ball. The end of the string whipped across and removed the leg bail. As if that was not bizarre enough, he was given out . . . . l.b.w.!

Cricket field architects must be among the most tolerant of men. Unlike their colleagues, who gouge spectacular cavities in Spanish hillsides and Japanese mountains, planting elegant golf courses in terrain previously fit for llamas, cricket field architects are by and large content to leave things as they find them. 'Run a mower over it,' they may say to a minion (if they can find one), 'but take it easy in the outfield. And for heaven's sake don't touch that oak tree. If God had not intended it to stand at short square leg, He would have got the bird to drop the acorn somewhere else.'

Trees are the biggest single cause of 'local rules', and it is a tribute to the variousness of club committees that each tree seems to be **festooned with unique laws.** Wincanton's tree is well inside the boundary, where a deep mid-off or closeish fine-leg would field. Batsmen may not be caught off it, and must run their runs (no free fours for hitting it).

At Great Baxted in Essex two trees stand just within the field of play and roughly square with the wicket. Perhaps because the trees are so near the boundary, any shot hitting one of them counts as four runs. Sixty years ago at Norton Hall, near Worcester, the batsmen were not so fortunate and could be caught off the tree. At Copford, near Colchester, a large mature oak tree stands within a few yards of the square. Our correspondent reporting its presence added that he had been unable to discover any local rules, and he presumed therefore that shots striking the tree would have to be run. To us this lack of information is mysterious, and the possibility cannot be ruled out that the home side may be keeping something up their sleeves. They have to be more precise in first-class cricket: on the St Lawrence ground at Canterbury the famous lime tree inside the field of play is considered part of the boundary.

Certainly, visiting teams do well to be on their guard when they play at grounds with unusual features inside the field of play. If the matter of local rules is not discussed and settled before play begins, the visitors have only themselves to blame if something is sprung on them later in the day. At Alveston, near Thornbury in Gloucestershire, the ground was situated to the rear of the Ship Hotel. A visiting batsman, with more than 70 to his credit, struck the ball high over the bowler's head. 'Six more,' he thought, as the ball landed on the **sloping roof of a cowshed,** the wall of which doubled as a sight-screen, bounced back into the field of play and was caught by a fielder. The batsman, to his surprise, was given out. Querying this with the umpire, he was told: 'You're out, zur. Oh, no zur, you're out! W. G. Grace caught a ball off that roof in 1886; he said it were out, and out it has been ever since!'

W. G.'s firmness on that small Gloucestershire club ground is proof among many that a star performer can be a law unto himself within the borders of his own county. Harry Jupp evidently thought so too. This great Surrey stalwart played for his county from 1862–81, and was renowned for his dislike of being dismissed. Playing in a minor match at Dorking – his native village – he was bowled first ball. He turned, picked up the bails, replaced them and resumed his stance. 'Ain't you going out, Juppy?' someone asked him. 'No,' said Jupp, 'not at Dorking I ain't.' And he didn't.

Greater flexibility was shown at Croxley Green, though **only after**

some bloodshed. There, on the ground of Old Merchant Taylors, several trees were included in the playing area, and around the base of one of them grew a particularly large and prickly hollybush.

In a match played a few years ago against Richmond Town, OMTs batted first and amassed 216, and although the visiting fielder among the trees had some difficulty in anticipating the rebounds, nothing untoward happened. In their reply Richmond Town had reached 90–3 when the ball was hit in the general direction of the trees. The batsmen had taken two comfortable runs when they realized that the ball had ended up in the heart of the hollybush. The fielders were as confused as the batsmen. While they tossed a coin to see who would retrieve the ball, the batsmen decided to cash in and started on a marathon run-gathering exercise. The count had reached six when the visiting umpire called: 'Dead ball'. This was overruled by the home umpire who immediately replied: 'No, carry on running. That tree is in the field of play.'

The batsmen restarted, had reached nine and were embarking on their tenth run when a scratched and bleeding hand emerged from the bush holding the ball. But for the delay by the batsmen on completion of the second run and the intervention of the visiting umpire, twelve could well have been scored from the one hit. Soon after the match the trees were excluded from the playing area – to general relief, though they remain a fond memory for a few lucky batsmen.

ACKNOWLEDGMENTS

The publishers would like to acknowledge with thanks
the help given by the following who supplied the
stories around which this book has been developed.

Qamar Ahmed, Bob Arrowsmith, Bish Barnard, Martin
Blackman, A.R. Borthwick, Mike Bray, Harry Brewer, R.T.
Brittenden, J.F. Burrell, Aubrey Bush, W.R. Chignell, John
Coffey, James D. Coldham, Anandji Dossa, A. Evans, Glen
Ewart, Peter George, Peter Hargreaves/Tom Provis,
Geoff Hayman, Roger Henderson, John Hollinshead, J.F.
Hyde Blake, C.D. Johnson, Quentin Jones, S.H.W. Levey,
C.E. Mansfield, Kersi Meher-Homji, George Mell, M.
Mervitz, Tony Moss, Keith Nicholas, R.C. Normandale,
G.C. Osborne, A.L. Parsons, S.S. Perera, George Pinney,
S.W. Rogers, J.G. Senior, Peter Snape (*Yorkshire Post*),
Eric Snow, Philip A. Snow (from *Cricket in the Fiji Islands*,
1949), John R. Swain, W. van Rossem, Frank Warwick,
James B. Wilson, Ron Wood, Reg Woodward.

The publishers also thank the following sources for
their help in providing illustrations:
BBC Hulton Picture Library, Central Press Photos Limited,
Patrick Eagar, Keystone, The Mansell Collection,
Marylebone Cricket Club.

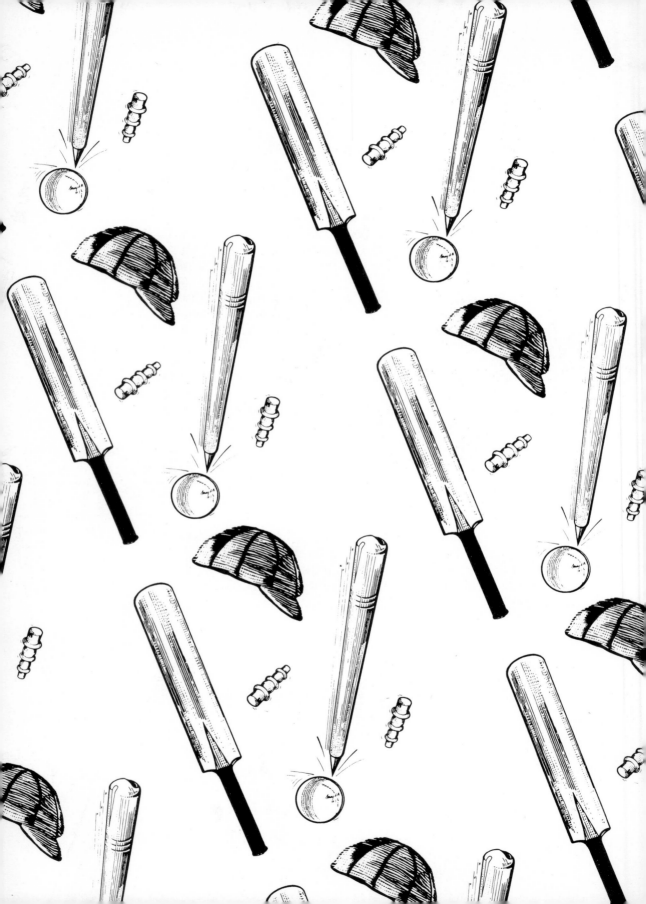

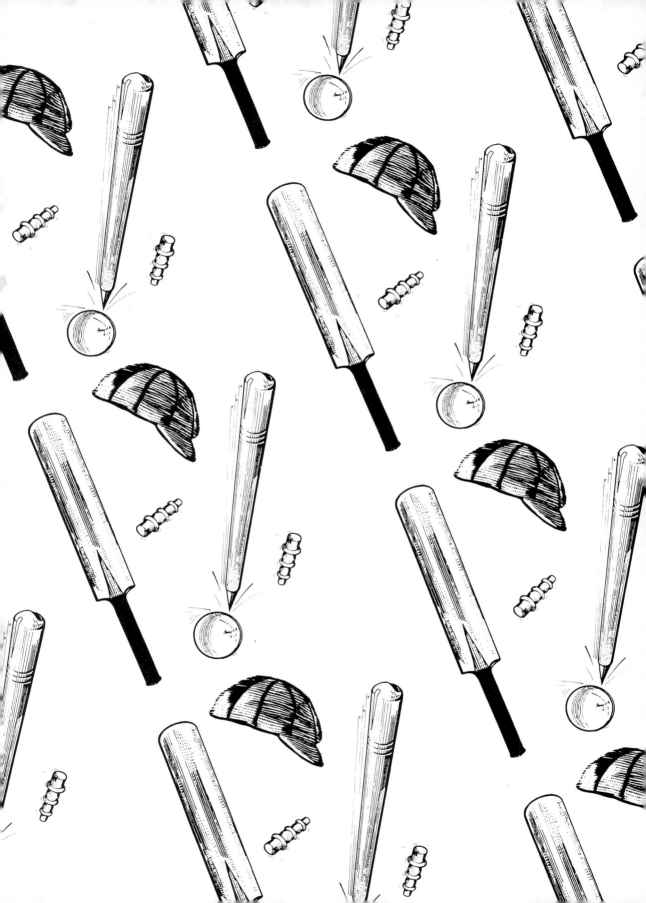